LIVING LOVE

In Conversation with
The No. 1 Ladies' Detective Agency
Series

LIVING LOVE

In Conversation with *The No. 1 Ladies' Detective Agency* Series

JOHN INGE

British Library Cataloguing in Publication data

A catalogue record for this book is available
from the British Library

ISBN 978-1-905958-04-7

First published by Inspire
4 John Wesley Road
Werrington
Peterborough PE4 6ZP

Typeset by Regent Typesetting, London
Printed and bound in Great Britain by
Stanley L. Hunt (Printers) Ltd, Rushden, Northants

For Denise, Eleanor and Olivia

Foreword

This wise and inspiring book encourages us to live good and godly lives. Bishop John, by examining the life of Mma Ramotswe, the heroine of Alexander McCall Smith's *The No. 1 Ladies' Detective Agency* series, reveals in a very practical way what makes for a good and godly life.

It is not by chance that some people are good and others bad. As Bishop John rightly points out, it is a matter of formation and choices. Good people choose to do the right things whatever the cost. The passion of good people is always to enrich and improve human relationships and what builds up the common life.

All good people, irrespective of race, culture, religion or nationality, have supremely in common the influence of religion on their lives. Their faith in God, handed down from generation to generation, is the key to their good and godly lives.

Mma Ramotswe, as you, the reader of this book, will come to realize, is a good and wise woman. Her faith in God, nurtured in the Church, Scriptures and good influence, sparkles in her thinking, words and deeds. She sees people through the eyes of God. As the psalmist said, 'In your light shall we see light.' This viewpoint exudes harmony in life. But when we lose this perspective and see people through the idols of wealth, materialism, technology or science, things fall apart.

The Africa of western media so widely publicized is where things fall apart. It is a depressing story of poverty, disease, wars and disasters. But the Africa of Mma Ramotswe is decent. People share the little they have in their poverty. There is a Setswana idiom that says, 'Bana ba motho ba kgaoganya tlhogo ya tsie', which literally translated means, 'A household share a head of a locust.' The Africa of Mma Ramotswe is where children respect their elders, and people live in hope of a better tomorrow. It is a place of humour and laughter where people have time to chat to each other; where some good leaders exist who have the interest of their people at heart; where economies are growing and corruption is lower than in some European countries. This Africa exists. And Mma Ramotswe's beloved country Botswana is a case in point.

We commend Alexander McCall Smith for drawing our attention to this neglected side of Africa which has so much good to teach the world about how we can live together as brothers and sisters. Mma Ramotswe epitomizes Botswana, a place where religions, ethnic groups, nationalities and races co-exist peacefully.

Alexander McCall Smith captures sensitively and knowingly the spirit and culture of Botswana in his books. He is not just a brilliant novelist who connects with the soul and pulse of Botswana but more significantly he is an African at heart. It is from the heart that he writes about a way of life that Botswana lives unconsciously.

Bishop John's insight is to see beyond this life a spiritual core as reflected in Mma Ramotswe's life. Beyond the good stories in the books lie deep eternal lessons to learn. The number one lesson is this: for us to live good and godly lives, like Mma Ramotswe, we need to live out the love of God by helping people with the problems in their lives. It's all about human relationships and how we should always strive to see beyond ourselves to help, affirm, care and love one another. This is possible with the awareness that we exist in God's world and all people are sacred. To borrow a few lines from Elizabeth Barrett Browning:

> Earth's crammed with heaven,
> And every common bush afire with God:
> But only he who sees, takes off his shoes;
> The rest sit round it and pluck blackberries.

With this recognition we can see the importance of spirituality in our lives. This is what defines Africa and Mma Ramotswe. Her inner life with God is what interprets all things. Perhaps we don't realize, as Bishop John reminds us, that, '. . . our inner life has as much to do with the way in which we perceive and react to people and places as any objective factors about the place itself'.

A good and godly life is an outward reflection of an inner life right with God. We have to love ourselves properly within before we can love others outwardly. Mma Ramotswe is a person in harmony with her inner world, the kingdom of God within her.

Out of this harmony springs empathy pivotal to Mma Ramotswe's outlook on life. And the facets of life are interpreted from this spiritual core; the virtuous life, suffering and evil; forgiveness and reconciliation; friendship, greatness; the here and hereafter; the whole divine drama.

Bishop John wisely reminds those of us living the fast-paced, task-oriented demands of the modern western lifestyle of the need to slow down to Mma

Ramotswe's pace in order to look inside our own hearts to achieve harmony. We are encouraged to reflect profoundly upon the Christian faith which, in the past, has given western society much of what is best today. In doing so, we will not only rediscover our inner life in God who is love, but also the passion to live out that love which tames the savageness in us and makes gentle the life of this world. This is the life of Mma Ramotswe. This is the lesson of living love in Bishop John's book. May you live love.

Rt Revd Trevor Mwamba
Bishop of Botswana
Gaborone
March 2007

Conversations:
Series Introduction

'Theological reflection' is a fashionable term among those doing any kind of theological education or training for ministry. It is not a phrase used a great deal in churches week by week, or in wider society. But 'theological reflection' is part of Christian discipleship. It is not something only for those who take up formal or authorized roles in churches. It is simply a way of referring to 'thinking about faith'. If Christians do not think about their faith, and fail to use the rich resources of the Christian tradition, then faith is not living, and may not actually be to do with God. Theological reflection is necessary precisely in order to ensure that God, rather than human ideas or beliefs about God, is at the heart of the faith professed.

If faith is not lively and thoughtful, people outside of churches have little reason to be interested. But how is such 'thinking about faith' prompted? How does 'theological reflection' actually happen? How can it occur in language that as many people as possible have a chance of understanding? And how, especially, can it occur in the middle of ordinary life, in the context of what people are actually doing anyway (working, being friends, trying to be a family, being entertained, engaging with the arts, practising sport, and so on)?

Conversations is a series of books which acknowledges that Christians are prompted to think about faith in many different ways. When we read novels, watch films or plays, listen to music or poetry, questions and insights arise which get us thinking. What we watch, read or listen to may or may not be from a Christian source. Sometimes we are given fresh insights by a Christian novelist. Sometimes we are challenged by a writer or a film-director who offers a direct critique of Christianity. 'Theological reflection' happens, though, the moment a work of art, or a media product (or sporting event, or life experience) invites deep thinking. The resources of a religious tradition can be brought to bear whenever questions about meaning, value or purpose arise in daily life. A 'conversation' then takes place between whatever has prompted the thinking, and the religion's ideas and beliefs. *Christian theology* happens, then, when a text or a film and the insights, convictions, statements of belief and doctrines that make up the Christian tradition come into conversation.

This series of books puts on paper a selection of 'conversations' that have been conducted by a number of contemporary Christians. All the contributors are people who are committed to the Church, knowledgeable about Christian tradition, and attuned to the complex but creative role that the arts and media play in society today. *Conversations* is therefore a series which recognizes that 'theological reflection' can start at a number of different places. One of the places it begins is with what we read, watch and listen to 'for fun', for interest, for enjoyment, whether or not we are looking for theological stimulus. The series shows, then, that 'theological reflection' can be done creatively and enjoyably by anyone prepared to ask questions about life and culture. Those who are willing to attend to, and wrestle with the questions and answers which go to and fro between life, the arts, broader culture and the Christian tradition *are* theologians. By showing what can happen in response to what we watch, listen to or read, *Conversations* plays its part in ensuring that creative theological thinking continues to be a part of a lively faith, a lively church and a lively, life-seeking, society.

Clive Marsh
Series Editor

The following abbreviated titles from the *No. 1 Ladies Detective Agency* series are used:

No. 1	*The No. 1 Ladies' Detective Agency*
Tears	*Tears of the Giraffe*
Company	*In the Company of Cheerful Ladies*
Morality	*Morality for Beautiful Girls*
Blue Shoes	*Blue Shoes and Happiness*
Kalahari	*The Kalahari Typing School for Men*
Full Cupboard	*The Full Cupboard of Life*

Extracts from *The No. 1 Ladies' Detective Agency* series by Alexander McCall Smith are reproduced by permission of Polygon, an imprint of Birlinn Ltd (www.birlinn.co.uk).

Acknowledgements

This book arose out of a love for the Christian gospel and for Africa, where I have been privileged to see it brought alive as nowhere else. I am very grateful to the many Christians in several countries of that great continent who have been an inspiration to me over many years, and to Alexander McCall Smith for his books, which speak so eloquently of it. I offer my thanks both to him and Bishop Trevor Mwamba for their encouragement in this project and to Natalie Watson and Clive Marsh, my editors, for their invitation to embark upon it, together with much helpful advice during its execution. The good influence of many others is present on every page. I single out particularly my gratitude to my colleague Bishop Anthony Russell and others in the Diocese of Ely. My profoundest thanks go to Denise and Eleanor and Olivia.

Contents

1

The Good Life

Alexander McCall Smith once saw a woman chasing a chicken around her yard in Botswana and at that moment he thought that he might write a book about a cheerful woman of 'traditional build'. Fifteen years after witnessing the scene she became the inspiration for Precious Ramotswe, founder of the first ladies' detective agency in Botswana. *The No. 1 Ladies' Detective Agency* and the series of books which followed have been hugely popular. Not only have they sold in their millions but the first book received two Booker Judges' Special Recommendations and was voted one of the 'International Books of the Year and the Millennium' by the *Times Literary Supplement*. I first came across them when I saw not one but two volumes in the series in the top 10 best sellers in a station bookstore: having bought one I was hooked. They are delightful, gripping and thought-provoking. They have received mixed reviews, some dismissing them as facile. Most, however, have concurred with the verdict of the millions who have bought them and recognized, with the *Spectator*, that 'for all their apparent simplicity, the Precious Ramotswe books are highly sophisticated'. Another review said of the first book that it is 'one of those rare, unassuming novels that seem to contain all of life within its pages, and affirms life in telling its story'. These books are

1

not anything like the usual representatives of the whodunit genre: whereas people die with alarming frequency in the average Agatha Christie or Ruth Rendell there are, by contrast, no great happenings in these pages – no murders, not even cosy ones. The purpose of the No. 1 Ladies' Detective Agency is clearly explained by Mma Ramotswe when she tells a client indignantly, 'We are not here to solve crimes. We help people with the problems in their lives.'

How we should live our lives is a crucial question which the Christian faith seeks to address. The intention of this book is to attempt a conversation between the Christian faith and the *No. 1 Ladies' Detective Agency* series because the latter sheds light on some of the deeper truths of the Christian faith and give insights into good and godly living in an uncomplicated and accessible manner. They also challenge Christians to look at their tradition by allowing their readers to come into contact with the latter through the medium of story, which is the manner in which Jesus challenged people to engage with truth and virtue. The Christian faith has story at its heart. Not only did Jesus himself communicate truth by parable, his entire life can be seen as the story of God's love for us. Thus, if someone were to ask me, as a Christian, what God is like, I would not want to begin by talking about the omnipotence, omnipresence and omniscience of God, important though these are. I would not see the need to resort to any theological or philosophical terminology but, rather, tell a story which would begin with something like: 'There was a man born in an obscure corner of the Middle East two thousand years ago.' This is because the story of the life, death and resurrection of Jesus Christ says more about the nature and love of God than any sophisticated theological discourse. That is not to say that the latter does not have its place: part of my reason for writing this book is to encourage readers to realize that theology can be accessible, interesting and deeply rewarding. Christian theology, though, is about reflecting upon that seminal story.

The first case to which we are introduced in the *No. 1 Ladies' Detective Agency* has the heroine doing just that. One of her early clients, Happy Bapetsi, comes to her because a man has appeared and told her that he was her father. Her father had left when she was a baby and she and her mother had presumed him to be dead, but then a man appeared on her door-step 'claiming to be her daddy' and asked whether he could stay with her since he had nowhere else to go. She welcomed him but, three months after waiting on him hand and foot, arrived at Mma Ramotswe's door because she had become suspicious – convinced, even – that he was not, in fact, her father (*No. 1*, 5ff.).

The 'traditionally built' (a wonderful and much used euphemism) proprietor of the detective agency springs into action. She borrows a nurse's uniform from a friend, squeezes herself into it, and drives to Happy Bapetsi's house in her tiny white van. She sweeps up to the gate and runs to the house, outside which the counterfeit father sits passing the time of day. He proudly asserts that he is Happy's father, whereupon she tells him that his daughter has suf-fered a very bad accident, that she needs a great deal of blood, and that only his blood, as a relative, will do. Sensing that this man is an impostor and her ruse will work, she goes on: 'That is why we are asking you, because she needs so much blood, they will have to take about half your blood. And that is very dangerous for you. In fact, you might die.' She tells him that she knows that he will do this thing for his daughter. He immediately crumples, confesses that he is not Happy's father, and Mma Ramotswe gives him five minutes to leave. She leaves a note for Happy Bapetsi which reads: 'That was not your Daddy after all. I found out the best way. I got him to tell me himself. Maybe you will find the real daddy one day. Maybe not. But in the meantime you can be happy again' (*No. 1*, 12).

This episode characterizes the heroine of these stories who is both good and wise. She finds ingenious methods to do the right thing and see justice prevail. Good wins out not through the exercise of power (except that of intellect, intuition and love, of which more later) and certainly not through the use of violence, but through the imagination and commitment of a good person. In fact, one could argue that her commitment to justice is not what it might be: the false daddy in the above account is allowed to get away without facing charges for his crime. Mma Ramotswe is generously disposed even towards those who have been the perpetrators of crimes.

The example of a good person

I think that a big part of the appeal of these books is that they are an attempt to tell stories about a good and a big-hearted person. As McCall Smith told an interviewer: 'These books are very non-aggressive, very gentle. They're quiet books, there's a lot of drinking of tea. They're about good people leading good lives.'[1] So much of current art tends to focus upon the

dark side of human nature, its pathological tenden-
cies, and fails to put before us the quality of goodness. Goodness is attractive, which is why the books
appeal. However, novels about good people who are
not just superhuman cardboard cut-outs have, since
the days of Jane Austen, been few and far between.
Where good people have appeared in fiction they
have often appeared to be rather weak and watery,
like Mr Harding in Anthony Trollope's *Barchester
Towers*. There is a fascination with fictional evil in
our society which perhaps stems from the fact that
in our childhood most of us developed an interest in
things we were not allowed to do and that, at that
age, 'being good' seemed rather tedious. At the same
time, however, there is nurtured in us an interest in
goodness as we are exposed to fairy tales and other
tales of virtue in which we see ourselves alongside
our heroes. These books are tales of virtue for adults
in which the characters who are good really 'live'
and, though they seem to fly in the face of what it has
been thought will sell, there is clearly a market for
them.

It is of note that the Greek word for 'good' which
Jesus uses when he describes himself as the 'Good
Shepherd' is also the word for 'beautiful'. Goodness
should be attractive and these novels suggest that
it can be. Tales of virtue work on the premise that
contemplation of the good is not only interesting but
can inspire good in us. The philosopher Iris Murdoch
observed that 'there is a place inside and outside religion for a sort of contemplation of the Good, not just
by dedicated experts but by ordinary people', that
directing attention away from ourselves to what she
termed 'a distant transcendent perfection, a source of
uncontaminated energy' could be 'a source of *new* and

quite undreamt of virtue'.[2] There is much opportunity for the contemplation of unfussy but costly goodness in these books.

Mma Ramotswe, we are told, learned about good and evil at Sunday school which she had attended every week without fail between the ages of 6 and 11. Under the guidance of the teacher, Mma Mothibi, 'she had experienced no difficulty in understanding that it was wrong to lie and steal, and kill other people'. Her teacher 'read the Bible to them and made them recite the Ten Commandments over and over again, and told them religious stories from a small blue book which she said came from London and was not available anywhere else in the country' (*No. 1*, 33). McCall Smith makes clear how devoted Mma Ramotswe was to truth and right even at the age of 10 by telling a charming story about how she had won first prize in a drawing competition. She had gone to Gaborone with the Principal of her school to receive the prize from the Minister of Education. When she saw her picture on display at the ceremony she had been appalled to see that a caption had been put underneath which read 'Cattle beside Dam', when in fact her picture was of goats. Frightened that she was to become 'a criminal, a perpetrator of fraud' she confesses to the Minister of Education that he cannot give her the prize for a mistake. He frowns, looks at the label and then tells her: 'They are the ones who have made a mistake. I also think those are goats. I do not think that they are cattle.' Presenting her with the prize, he announces that it is an excellent picture of goats and whispers to her, 'You are the most truthful child I have ever met. Well done' (*No. 1*, 41).

Mma Ramotswe's goodness and wisdom come, in part at least, from her association with the Christian Church and her immersion in its Scriptures from an early age. Those of us who are familiar with the latter will immediately find in the story of Happy Bapetsi resonances of King Solomon's judgement concerning two women who shared a house and who claimed to be the mother of a baby (1 Kings 3.16–28). Both had given birth but one of the babies had died in the night and each of the women claimed that hers was the surviving child. Solomon directed that, since they could not agree, the living child should be cut in two and half given to one woman and half to the other. At this, the first woman, the mother of the living child, moved with love for her child, exclaimed that the baby should be given to the other woman. Solomon responded, 'Give the living baby to the first woman, do not kill it. She is its mother.' It is this story that is told in the Bible in order to demonstrate the wisdom of Solomon and the good purposes to which he puts that wisdom – nothing fancy but a very recognizable and useful form of practical wisdom used to enable good to prevail.

The virtuous life and the Christian Scriptures

If we are not able to make the connection between Happy Bapetsi and the wisdom of Solomon for ourselves, McCall Smith does it for us by giving us an insight into Mma Ramotswe's thought processes after she had assured Happy that she would solve the mystery. Having discounted to herself the possibility of a blood test we read that she stopped in her line of thought: 'Yes, there was something biblical about this story. What, she thought, would Solomon have done?'

In making the association explicit the author does at least two things. First, he makes it clear that the hero of the story has the same sort of down-to-earth wisdom as Solomon. Second, he intimates how Mma Ramotswe is so immersed in the Christian Scriptures that she is not just familiar with them: they have become so deeply embedded in her being that the manner in which she lives is formed by them. The Christian Scriptures shape her life as she applies them to it.

Tom Wright has suggested that the Christian life can be compared to taking part in an unfinished Shakespeare play. [3] He asks us to imagine that there exists such a play whose fifth act has been lost. The first four acts provide a great deal of characterization and such excitement within the plot that there is enthusiasm for the play to be staged. However, rather than leaving everyone guessing after the fourth act, or asking someone to write a fifth act, it is decided to give the key parts to expert actors who would be told to immerse themselves in the first four acts and in the language and culture of Shakespeare and his time and then work out the last act by themselves, to improvise it. This is the manner, he tells us, in which we might approach the Christian life. We have the Scriptures and we have the Christian tradition. They will not tell us exactly what we ought to do in any given instance but they will be the bedrock upon which we are called to improvise. This improvisation will be both conscious and unconscious since, as I have suggested above, some of the most important moral decisions we make are ones about which we do not have to stop and think. Mma Ramotswe is a fine example of such improvisation: she uses what she has learned from her Christian formation and the gifts God has given her, of intelligence and common sense, to enable her to do the right thing. A manual on how to be a detective which Mma Ramotswe purchases advises one to pay attention to hunches. 'Hunches are another form of knowledge' (*No. 1*, 79). Doing what *feels* right will, in other words, be a safe guide to doing what is right if we have been immersed from an early age in a community where right and wrong are clearly distinguished, as she had.

Shouldn't ethics be concerned with laying down clear guidelines about what is right and what is wrong? There is a place for this, as the learning of the Ten Commandments by Mma Ramotswe makes clear, but the fact is that not every eventuality will be covered by them in a straightforward manner. We should remember, too, that Jesus himself, as well as telling stories and allowing people to draw their own conclusions from them, was forever asking questions and seldom answered them. In the gospels he asks 307 questions. He is asked 183 questions himself, directly or indirectly and only answers three of them straightforwardly. To the others he gives no response, changes the subject, asks another question, tells a story, or says that it is the wrong question. The only thing on which he concentrates insistently is the goodness and reliability of God. The three questions that he answers directly are first, whether or not he is a king, to which he replies in the affirmative, though clarifying what 'king' means in this context (John 18.33ff.); second, the request from his disciples to be taught to pray, to which he gives them the Lord's Prayer (Luke 11.1ff.) and, third, 'Which commandment is the first of all?' To this he replies, ". . . You shall love the Lord your God with all your heart, and with all your soul, and with all your mind, and with all your strength". The second is this, "You shall love your neighbour

as yourself." There is no other commandment greater
than these' (Mark 12.28 ff.).

In the above instance we see Jesus improvising
upon the law in order to provide us with the bedrock
upon which our lives should be built. However, we
ourselves need to improvise in order to apply that
bedrock. In theatre to improvise is to carry the action
forward in a manner which is true to what has gone
before. Professional actors who improvise do so
according to dramatic guidelines which keep them
faithful to the plot, using their training as actors to
help them to decide how to act in any situation. We
must do the something similar in our lives using the
Christian Scriptures and tradition as our guide. Mma
Ramotswe gives us a fine example of how this can
be done and we receive further inspiration through
the insights we are given in the books into what has
formed her.

Formed in love

We know that Precious Ramotswe has become a
good person through her formation by the Christian
Scriptures but also by her experience of other people
who have lived out the truths found in them. She is
the daughter of Obed Ramotswe, described as a 'good
man'. Her mother was killed by a train when she was
four, after which she was cared for by Obed's cousin,
whose husband had left her because she was barren.
The author implies that this cousin loved Precious
greatly, as did her adoring father, so that she was
surrounded by love in her childhood. In her case it is
true to say that her family was her first experience of

'church' in that it acted as an early school of love, with mealtimes as its liturgy. Mma Ramotswe articulates something similar in *Tears of the Giraffe*:

> God had been kind to her, thought Mma Ramotswe. He had given her a happy childhood, even if her mother had been taken from her when she was a baby. She had been looked after by her father and her kind cousin and they had taught her what it was to give love – love which she had in turn given, over those few precious days, to her tiny baby. When the child's battle for life had ended, she had briefly wondered why God had done this to her, but in time she had understood. Now his kindness to her was manifest again, this time in the appearance of Mr J.L.B. Matekoni, a good, kind man. God had sent her a husband. (*Tears*, 5)

Jesus tells us to think of God as our Father. This will help us if our own father has been as attentive and loving as was Obed Ramotswe to his daughter. Sadly, many fathers in western society today are absent from their children. Love can, however, be communicated and learned through people other than biological parents, as was the case with Precious Ramotswe's experience with her cousin. Receiving love helps us to give it, as it did Mma Ramotswe.

The cousin not only cared for Precious, she wanted her to be clever. She taught her to count and also played a variety of Kim's Game in which she would load a basket-work tray with familiar objects and then drape a blanket over it and remove one object. We read that 'she was never wrong, this child who watched everybody and everything with her wide, solemn eyes. And slowly, without anybody ever having intended this, the qualities of curiosity and awareness were nurtured in the child's mind' (*No. 1*, 31). The cousin stayed until Precious was eight, at which point she left to be married again, leaving the little girl with a note to say that 'I know that you are missing me, but I know that you want me to be happy. I am very happy now . . . Now you must look after your father, as you are old enough to do that, and he is a good man too. I want you to be happy and that is what I pray for, every night. God look after Precious Ramotswe. God watch her tonight and forever. Amen' (*No. 1*, 38).

Having been formed in love and wisdom Mma Ramotswe uses both to good effect in her adult life through imaginative improvisation: the story of how she tricked the man who was pretending to be Happy Bapetsi's father into a confession illustrates this well. On many occasions in the books she goes far beyond the finding of information as a private detective: she works tirelessly in order to see good prevail. In a number of her successful cases, she muses to herself in *Tears of the Giraffe*:

> She had made decisions about the outcome, and these decisions had often proved to be momentous ones, For example, in the case of the woman whose husband had stolen a Mercedes Benz, she had arranged for the return of the car to its owner. In the case of the fraudulent insurance claims by the man with thirteen fingers, she had made the decision not to report him to the police. That was a decision which had changed a life. He

may have become honest after she had given him this chance, but he may not. She could not tell. But what she did was to offer him a chance, and that may have made a difference. So she did interfere in other people's lives, and it was not true that all she did was provide information. (*Tears*, 159)

The role of the church

In seeking to lead the good life it is not only our formation but the company we keep that is crucial. This is part of the role of churches: they provide a setting in which Christians can be encouraged by one another's fellowship and example. As such they are 'communities of virtue' in which people are able to be alongside one another, supporting one another in living godly and good lives. Churches do not have a monopoly on this, of course, but they are unique in providing a context in which people not only meet one another but actively seek the aid of God's Holy Spirit to assist them in leading good lives.

When they meet in church, and at other times, Christians consult the primary 'instruction manual' on the good and godly life, the Bible. Though the Scriptures always retain priority as the inspired word of God, other writings can be helpful. Among them will be biblical commentaries and theological books, as well as lives of the saints, which function as 'tales of virtue' as I have described them above. What is not often recognized is the power of the novel. There is always a temptation to say of novels that they are 'only fiction'. However, it is crucial to appreciate the power of story, which Jesus used to such good and memorable effect. Much truth is found in fiction. When Jesus told the parables of the Good Samaritan and the Prodigal Son, someone might have asked him, after he had told one of these stories, whether or not it was true. 'What do you mean by true?' Jesus might have responded. 'Well, did it actually happen?' To ask this latter question is to betray a great lack of understanding of the richness of truth. Stories which have no grounding in historical fact can be a powerful and profound means of conveying the deepest truths. Truth can be mediated by fiction, sometimes very powerfully, and these novels are a case in point.

We are told that Mma Ramotswe, like half of Botswana, 'thought the church way'. It could only be a result of her immersion in church and in a profoundly Christian culture that she 'thought the church way'. As we see in the novels, she certainly acted the church way, improvising upon the Scriptures and all that she had learned through the church in order to live out the good life. In these books McCall Smith is giving us a potentially very helpful resource for reflecting upon how we might do the same. They are not equivalent to the Christian gospel, of course, but they do have the potential to encourage Christians to rediscover the truth and power of that gospel. There is a pressing need for such a rediscovery and for its articulation to western society, which is in danger of forgetting its roots. The Archbishop of York recently intervened in arguments which have been raging in England over what is seen as the suppression of Christmas by such terms as 'winterval'. He issued a press release which included the following words:

> Why don't the aggressive secularists and illiberal atheists listen to the great wisdom of

Sir John Mortimer, playwright and atheist, who writing in the *Daily Telegraph* on 28th April 1999 said: 'Our whole history and culture in Europe is based on Christianity, whether you believe in it or not. Our culture is Christian; Shakespeare, Mozart – all that makes life worth living is part of the Christian tradition.'[4]

Whilst Christians should have respect for other faiths, they should not be apologetic in pointing out that most of what is best in western society is associated with the Christian faith. In 1949 Churchill proclaimed that 'there is no hope for the world unless the peoples of Europe unite together to preserve their freedom, their culture and their civilization founded on Christian ethics'.[5] It is interesting that nowadays it takes an archbishop who was born and raised in Africa to make similar points. In the same vein, in 1998 the former Bishop of Zanzibar and Archbishop of Tanzania, John Ramadhani, preached in Ely Cathedral (Ely Cathedral and Zanzibar Cathedral are linked). He surprised the congregation by thanking them – thanking them for the fact that their forbears had brought to Africa the Christian faith, from which he and countless other Africans had benefited so much.

These novels, set in Africa, can serve as a reminder that the ethical system of western society stems from the Christian faith. Having been so reminded, and having reflected theologically upon them, Christians will be better equipped to speak to an amnesiac society about its Christian heritage. In the next chapter I shall look at the most pressing of difficulties facing all people of faith, that of suffering and evil, and what encouragement the *No. 1 Ladies' Detective Agency* series can give in thinking theologically about them so as to live and witness to the Christian life in the face of them.

2

Suffering and Evil

Mma Ramotswe walked back towards her
van, not wanting to intrude upon the intimate
moments of reunion. She was crying, for her
own child, too – remembering the minute hand
that grasped her own, so briefly, while it tried
to hold on to a strange world that was slipping
away so quickly. There was so much suffering
in Africa that it was tempting to shrug your
shoulders and walk away. But you can't do that,
she thought. You just can't. (*No. 1*, 221)

So reflects Mma Ramotswe, having tracked down a
10-year-old boy who had been kidnapped and reunited
him with his father, as she watches him stumble forward to seize his son, and hold him, while he shouted
wildly, incoherently, for the village and the world
to hear his joy. Though they present a world which
is, in one sense, uncomplicated, these books do not
give the pretence that life is free from suffering. Far
from it. As I have already intimated, Mma Ramotswe
learns early not only of love but of the pain of loss.
We are not given any insight into the grief she experienced at the death of her mother or at her cousin's
departure but are left to imagine the agony. There
was much more suffering to come. When she was 16
'she wanted to go somewhere, she wanted her life to

start' so her father suggested to her that she should go to the cousin who had cared for her because, as he put it, 'that is a very different place. I think you will find lots of things happening in that house.' She leaves home to live with the cousin and works in the office of her husband's bus company. She works hard and, being very bright, soon discovers that one of the other two clerks is defrauding his employer. Dealing with this, we are told, was the beginning of her career. She spends four years working for her cousin's husband, during which she meets Note Mokoti, a philandering jazz musician, to whom she is fatally attracted. She marries him, but is badly abused by him before she bears their child who dies when only a few days old. She returns to her father when Note deserts her and 'there she stayed, looking after her father, for the next fourteen years. He died shortly after her thirty-fourth birthday, and that was the point at which Precious Ramotswe, now parentless, veteran of a nightmare marriage, and mother, for a brief and lovely five days, became the first lady private detective in Botswana' (*No. 1*, 55).

Enlarging hearts through empathy

We are presented with suffering as a fact of life in these books. It is rendered all the more affecting by the understated manner in which it is introduced. We do not learn a great deal more about the death of her child than in that last sentence but we feel for her and can thereby identify a little more easily, perhaps, with the millions of mothers who face the death of their children in the vast continent of Africa. It is easier to open our hearts to individuals than it is to statistics. Horrifying statistics about enormous numbers of people suffering can sometimes cause us either to despair or to turn our backs and cease to care. In these books, though, statistics are translated into the stories of the lives of people with whom we can empathize. As such, the books develop our moral imagination. The potential of the phenomenon of empathy lies at the heart of these books. Its importance is articulated when Mma Ramotswe is considering a friend who treated her maid badly and reflects that

> such behaviour was no more than ignorance; an inability to understand the hopes and aspirations of others. That understanding . . . was the beginning of all morality. If you knew how a person was feeling, if you could imagine yourself in her position, then surely it would be impossible to inflict further pain. Inflicting pain in such circumstances would be like hurting oneself. (*Morality*, 77)

Empathy is not something upon which Christians are often encouraged to reflect. It is not listed as one of the fruits of the Spirit by the apostle Paul: love, joy, peace, patience, kindness, faithfulness, gentleness and self-control (Galatians 5.22–23). These are all closely related to empathy but they are not equivalent to it. Empathy, however, lies right at the heart of the Christian faith. Paul tells us that Jesus, 'though he was in the form of God . . . emptied himself, taking the form of a slave, being born in human likeness' (Philippians 2.6–7). As a result, as the author of the letter to the Hebrews can proclaim: 'We do not have a high priest who is unable to sympathize with our weaknesses, but we have one who in every respect has been tested as we are, yet without sin. Let us therefore approach the throne of grace with boldness, so that

we may receive mercy and find grace to help in time
of need' (Hebrews 4.15–16). In other words: fear not,
God in Christ *empathizes* with us. If we are called to
improvise in order to lead godly lives then empathy
will be a crucial tool in developing our moral imagination and enabling us to do so. By making clear the
power of empathy these books offer Christians an
important and challenging insight into the truths that
lie at the heart of their faith. We hear of compassion
in Christian circles but compassion can, like charity, tend to imply a distance, suggesting that one is
'looking down', albeit benignly, upon someone else.
Christ, however, 'emptied himself' and responded to
the needs of another as an equal. Christians, enlarg-
ing their hearts through empathy, are called to do the
same.

It is through developing our empathy with individuals that McCall Smith introduces us to some of
the pains of Botswana. We learn, in moving detail,
of how Mma Ramotswe's father, like so many others, left Bechuanaland Protectorate, as Botswana was
then called, at the age of 18 to work in the mines in
South Africa. Obed recounts: 'the women cried and
we waved good-bye. Young men always try not to cry
or look sad, but I knew that within us all our hearts
were sad' (*No. 1*, 13ff.). We learn thereafter of the
cruelty they all suffered. When, at the age of 60, Obed
Ramotswe learns that he has not long to live, he refers
to the old Sotho song, 'The mines eat men. Even when
they have left you, the mines may still be eating you.'
The terrible injustices inflicted upon so many for so
long in Africa come alive for us by virtue of the fact
that we have already developed an affection for this
man, Obed Ramotswe, and his daughter.

We are introduced similarly to Botswana's continuing dominant tragedy, HIV/AIDS. Though the country is, economically, one of the most successful in Africa and, socially and politically, one of the most stable, it has one of the highest incidences of HIV/AIDS on the continent. There are only a few references to this in the books. As McCall Smith told an interviewer: 'The Botswanans themselves don't dwell on it. They just wish to continue with their ordinary lives as best they can, and as far as possible I want to respect their wishes. They don't talk about it all the time – they're obviously sensitive about it – so there's no reason why I should.'[1] So, the author 'tells it slant' by introducing us to the pain of its ravages in a particular situation. We learn of its devastating effect through the brother of Mma Makutsi, Mma Ramotswe's assistant, whom she had nursed during the final months of his life in a small corner of her one room which she had curtained off for his sickbed and had nursed him,

> doing her best to make him comfortable in the morning before she went off for work, and bringing him whatever small delicacies she could afford from her meagre salary. They had told her to make sure that he ate even if his appetite was tiny . . . But none of this – none of the special food, the nursing or the love which she so generously provided, could alter the dreadful truth that the disease which was making his life so hard could never be beaten. It could be slowed down, or held in check, but it would always assert itself in the long run. (*Full Cupboard*, 70)

We learn of the sexism endemic in African society through the prejudice Mma Ramotswe faces. For example, when setting up her business she goes to see a lawyer who had arranged for the sale of her father's cattle. He suggests that women cannot be detectives. The ensuing conversation is worth quoting in full because it demonstrates another great strength of the books, their humour:

> 'Why not?' said Mma Ramotswe. She had heard that people did not like lawyers, and now she thought she could see why. This man was so certain of himself, so utterly convinced. What had it to do with him what she did? It was her money, her future. And how dare he say that about women, when he didn't even know that his zip was half undone! Should she tell him?
>
> 'Women are the ones who know what's going on,' she said quietly. 'They are the ones with eyes. Have you not heard of Agatha Christie?'
>
> The lawyer looked taken aback. 'Agatha Christie? Of course I know her. Yes, that is true. A woman sees more than a man sees. That is well known.'
>
> 'So,' said Mma Ramotswe, 'When people see a sign saying No. 1 Ladies' Detective Agency, what will they think? They'll think those ladies will know what is going on. They're the ones.'
>
> The lawyer stroked his chin. 'Maybe.'

'Yes,' said Mma Ramotswe. 'Maybe.'
Adding, 'Your zip, Rra. I think you may not
have noticed . . .'. (*No. 1*, 57)

There is nothing preachy about the hero of these
books but the goodness of Precious Ramotswe,
formed by the Christian Scriptures, shines through
them. Through her own suffering, she is enabled to
empathize with the suffering of others. It is sometimes remarked that suffering can be either ennobling
or embittering. Most of us will have met people for
whom it is possible to speak of suffering having been
ennobling. From a Christian perspective, suffering
can do more than ennoble, it can redeem. What I
mean by this is that God can bring good out of suffering. This is certainly true of Mma Ramotswe.
What we see emerging from her suffering is a good
person whose subsequent actions and relationships
are inspirational.

Empathy – and the dangers of a lack of it – is
sometimes referred to in unusual circumstances in
the books. Mma Ramotswe visits the mother of her
former husband, now an old and sick woman, and we
read that

> [t]he old woman said nothing for a moment,
> and Mma Ramotswe kept her arm about
> her shoulder. It was a strange feeling, she
> had always thought; feeling the breathing
> of another, a reminder of how we all share
> the same air, and of how fragile we are.
> At least there was enough air in the world
> for everyone to breathe; at least people did
> not fight with one another over that. And
> it would be difficult, would it not, for the
> rich people to take all the air away from the

poor people, even if they could take so many other things. Black people, white people: same air. (*Company*, 171)

In these books we learn to empathize with different groups of people who have suffered and are suffering through the stories of individuals. We are thereby encouraged to care in the manner commended by a housemother at Mma Potokwani's orphan farm who explains to Motholeli, 'We must look after other people . . . Other people are our brothers and sisters. If they are unhappy, then we are unhappy. If they are hungry, then we are hungry' (*Tears*, 124).

What is emphasized is the fundamental sameness of the human condition. A recognition of how much we have in common with people in very different situations will make empathy easier. Several reviewers have criticized McCall Smith for daring, being British, white and male, to write books in which the heroine is a black African woman. For example, Natalie Reeve writes:

In using black Africans to represent a simpler and better way of life, McCall Smith denies them respect and dignity. The attitude to black African men (foolish, often cheating on their wives and even physically abusing them) could be wry and self-deprecating in the hands of a black male writer – but coming from a white author it seems dangerously close to stereotype and even racism, albeit unintentional. I would be much happier if these books were written by a black African, rather than a settler of European origin (McCall Smith was born and raised in Zimbabwe). Then, rather than having an imitation of the style of traditional African folktales, we would have the genuine article: black Africans expressing their way of life on their own terms, and in their own voice.[2]

Reeve tells us that 'she would be much happier' if these books were written by a black African. She seems to be unaware of the fact that it is the skill of a good novelist to 'get under the skin' of people of different gender and culture and not to be confined by his or her own. (We would be rather short on Shakespeare plays if those set anywhere other than London or Stratford were to be expunged.) Maybe McCall Smith knows Botswana and is able to cross cultural boundaries with such ease that Reeve has forgotten that these are novels and not documentaries.

There are complex issues here, as any social anthropologist will testify, but as in the passages above, McCall Smith is showing us through the medium of the novel the power and the importance of empathy across cultural boundaries. Most of his readers will never know at first hand what it is like to have one's father die of a lung disease contracted in a South African mine, what it is like to live in a country afflicted by AIDS in quite the way Botswana is at present, what it is, as an African woman, to suffer the sexism of some African men (I say 'some' because not all the men in the novels are tarred with this brush). But we understand what it is to suffer and in these books we can have our moral imagination stretched to the point that we can empathize with those who suffer in these particular ways. If, at the same time, we can be encouraged to reflect upon the Christian inheritance of faith which has given western society much of what is best in it by engaging with people,

albeit fictional, in a country where it has taken hold
and still represents the norm, McCall Smith will have
achieved something very worthwhile in addition to
'a good read'. These books have been welcomed by
millions of people all over the world (including Botswana, where people say that they portray life there
very well) and I hope that this present volume might
help them to achieve more of their theological potential in encouraging and enabling the good life.

God and suffering

Seeing how good can emerge from suffering is not the
same as explaining how it can exist in the creation
of a loving God. Understanding suffering is more
of a problem for those who believe in a loving God
than those who do not since, in a world that emerged
simply by accident, anything goes and suffering is
'just the way things are'. On the other hand, explaining goodness is a problem for the atheist. Here is a
woman who, having suffered so much, is still reso-
lutely committed to the good, the right and the true
even if it would not appear to be to her advantage.
The question of where this goodness comes from is
a difficult one for the atheist since it has no place in
a survival-of-the fittest or selfish-gene understanding
of the world.

The scientist and theologian John Polkinghorne,
who gave up being Professor of Theoretical Physics at
Cambridge University in order to train for ordination
in the Church of England, comments on attempts to
explain love and truth by genetic imprinting or tacit
cultural agreement. He feels that there is some truth
in these approaches but does not think that they

come anywhere near an adequate account of what is involved. He suggests that parental care for young children doubtless has a genetic element of passing on inheritance to future generations but that this does not explain such moving cases as that of a father who wished to donate his second kidney to a son who already had his own children, because the first transplant had failed. The father was, in effect, giving up his life for his son. Similarly, did Oskar Schindler take great risks to rescue more than a thousand Jews from extermination because of some implicit calculation of genetic advantage? Polkinghorne points out that the very fact that some peoples are reputed by anthropologists to have a selfish nature (he mentions the Ik tribe of East Africa) is interesting since they only receive publicity due to the atypical character of their morality. It is very unlikely that ethical acts are simply the result of cultural determination.[3]

The atheist Richard Dawkins has written that 'If the universe were just electrons and selfish genes, meaningless tragedies like the crashing of a bus are exactly what we should expect, along with equally meaningless *good* fortune. Such a universe would be neither evil nor good in intention. It would manifest no intentions of any kind. In a universe of blind genetic replication, some people are going to get hurt and other people are going to get lucky, and you won't find any rhyme or reason to it, nor any justice.'[4] Polkinghorne comments that whatever this bleak judgement is, it is clearly not a conclusion of science alone. The fact that human beings alone in creation can rebel against the tyranny of selfish replicators and overcome genetic programming in order to show altruism and goodness is not properly explained by atheists like Dawkins.

Interestingly, in McCall Smith's books, genes are mentioned to produce a rather different conclusion. In *The Morality of Beautiful Women*, Mma Makutsi relates an article she has read in *National Geographic* about the anthropologist Richard Leaky, which shows that the human species originated in East Africa. Mma Ramotswe asks, 'so we are all brothers and sisters, in a sense?' To which Mma Makutsi replies, 'We are. . . . We are all the same people. Eskimos, Russians, Nigerians. They are the same as us. Same blood. Same DNA.' The passage continues:

> Mma Ramotswe considered the implications of these revelations for a moment. She had no views on Eskimos and Russians but Nigerians were a different matter. But Mma Makutsi was right, she reflected: if universal brotherhood – and sisterhood – meant anything, it would have to embrace the Nigerians as well.
>
> 'If people knew this,' she said, 'if they knew that we were all from the same family, [would] they be kinder to one another, do you think?'
>
> Mma Makutsi put down the magazine. 'I'm sure they would,' she said. 'If they knew that, then they would find it very difficult to do unkind things to others. They might even want to help them a bit more.' (*Morality*, 11)

The insights of science are here blended with a firm belief in God as creator in order to produce a powerful encouragement to good living and the recognition that God is quite capable of working through evolution; and it strengthens the biblical insight that we are all brothers and sisters.

God and evil

Fyodor Dostoevsky grappled with the problem of suffering and belief in a good and loving God in his novel *The Brothers Karamazov*. There is a famous scene within that book where the two brothers, Ivan and Alyosha, who are then in their early twenties, meet at the monastery at which Alyosha is a novice. Ivan explains how he cannot accept the God whom Alyosha serves because of the terrible suffering and evil with which the world is filled. He talks of instances of terrible cruelty – Turks blowing out the brains of a baby in front of its mother with evident pleasure, a child who, having injured a general's favourite hound, is torn to pieces by the hounds in front of his mother. He explains that it is not that he does not accept God, it is just that he 'most respectfully returns Him the ticket'.

Dostoevsky does not answer directly the question of how God can allow such suffering. Rather, he places alongside it the life of Alyosha, a good person who was dedicated to a life of love. A similar approach is taken by the Revd Trevor Mwamba, a real person who is now Bishop of Botswana, in the course of a sermon on mystery which Mma Ramotswe hears preached in Gaborone Cathedral:

> If we look about our world today, if we look about this dear home of ours, Africa, then what do we see but tears and sorrow? Yes, we see those, we see those even in Botswana, where we are fortunate in so many ways.

We see this in the faces of those who are ill, in their fear and their sorrow at the thought that their lives will be so shortened. This is real suffering, but it is not suffering that we as Christians walk away from. Every day, every moment of our lives there are people who are working to alleviate this suffering. They are working at this task right now as I speak. Right across the road in Princess Marina Hospital, there are doctors and nurses working. There are our own people from far away, from America, for example, who are working to bring relief to those who are very sick from this cruel illness that stalks Africa. Do those people talk about such sufferings as proof that there can be no divine presence in this world? They do not. They do not ask that question. And many are sustained by that very faith at which some clever people like to sneer. And that, my friends, is the true mystery at which we should marvel. That is what we should think of in silence for a moment, as we remember the names of those who are ill, those members of this body, this Anglican church, our brothers and sisters. And I read them out now. (*Company*, 29)

In Mma Ramotswe McCall Smith presents us with one such person whose goodness is as impressive as the suffering she encounters is appalling. Through her we are reminded that good need not be eliminated from this admittedly cruel and pain-riddled world and can encourage us in working for the good against suffering. She empathizes with the suffering of others as a result of her own suffering and does not despair but sets about doing something about it. As she sat in the Anglican Cathedral waiting for the service to begin on that Sunday morning when Trevor Mwanza was preaching, she observes the list of the sick noting, with sorrow, that many of those who had been on the list last week were still named.

> It was a time of sickness, and charity was sorely tested. There were mothers here, mothers who would leave children behind them if they were called. There were rich people, too, all equal in their human vulnerability. Remember these brothers and sisters it said at the bottom of the list. Yes, she would, she would remember these brothers and sisters. How could one forget? (*Company*, 35)

Suffering and oppression are not avoided in these novels as we confront the personal pain of Mma Ramotswe and others and the communal scourge of such things as poverty and HIV/AIDS. However, such suffering and oppression is always placed alongside the goodness of the hero of these novels, who works tirelessly against it. What she can achieve is very limited but it is the very fact that she refuses to be ground down but, rather, continually chips away at it, that is inspiring. Virtue, we are reminded, is about the little choices we make for good, however overwhelming might be the evil with which we are surrounded. The heroine of these stories is not the only good person involved in them: other main characters, including Mr J.L.B. Matekoni and Mma Potokwani, who runs what is referred to as an orphan farm', are people whose lives are dedicated to the good in unspectacular but meaningful ways.

There is something magnetically attractive about this goodness which endures and develops in the face of suffering.

As Mma Ramotswe mused in the scene I quoted at the beginning of this chapter: 'There was so much suffering in Africa that it was tempting to shrug your shoulders and walk away. But you can't do that, she thought. You just can't' (*No. 1*, 221). The suffering of Africa is appallingly acute. The first time I visited a hospital in East Africa I and those who were with me were reduced to silence by virtue of how poorly equipped it was. Those going into it were very unlikely to be cured and much more likely only to contract further infections and so have their demise hastened. What made it all the more poignant was the knowledge that this was a pattern that was repeated all over Africa which Mother Teresa of Calcutta – another person whose witness in the face of tremendous suffering is inspirational – once described as a 'vast open calvary'.

To make things worse, much of the terrible suffering of Africa is not caused by natural factors but is the direct result of human evil. There is plenty of food in the world to ensure that no one should go hungry: famines and lack of medical care are caused by warfare, greed, neglect and indifference. Much of the suffering encountered by Mma Ramotswe is the result of human evil – from the illness of her father as a result of his exploitation in the mines of South Africa to the barbaric treatment she received at the hands of her husband, Note. Though the terrible scourge of HIV/AIDS has claimed huge numbers of innocent victims, the suffering inflicted by it is recognized in these books as being related to promiscuity. In a powerful passage Mma Ramotswe says:

> 'Ever since women allowed men to think that they did not need to get married, every-thing has gone wrong. That is what I think, Mma.' Poppy thought for a moment. 'I think you may be right,' she said. 'Look at the mess. Look at what all this unfaithfulness has done. People are dying because of that, aren't they? Many people are dying.' For a moment the three of them were silent. There was no gainsaying what Poppy had just said. It was true. Just true. (*Blue Shoes*, 36)

Redemption in Christ

The suffering of the twentieth century, much of it caused by human evil, was enormous and it continues. Such immensity of suffering has caused Christians to ask with renewed vigour that haunting question, where is God in all this? How can a good God allow such things? How can he stand by and see it happen? This question is answered quite starkly by Elie Wiesel, a survivor of Auschwitz, in his book *Night*:

> The SS hanged two men and a youth in front of the whole camp. The men died quickly, but the death throes of the youth lasted for half an hour. 'Where is God?' Where is he?' someone asked behind me. As the youth still hung in torment in the noose after a long time, I heard the man call again, 'Where is God now?' And I heard a voice in myself answer: 'Where is he? He is here. He is hanging on the gallows . . .'[5]

The above is quoted by Jürgen Moltmann in his book *The Crucified God*. Moltmann, himself a prisoner of war from 1945–48, is one of the most creative theologians of our time. We have seen above (p. 19) how the letter to the Hebrews makes clear that, through his incarnation, God in Christ is able to empathize with our weaknesses. Christian theology goes further, though, in suggesting that, far from being some impartial observer of the suffering of the world, God in Christ takes it upon himself in order to redeem it.

The Bible and Christian tradition use a range of metaphors when talking of what God did through the cross of Christ. These include 'redemption', 'salvation' and 'deliverance'. Paul speaks of 'justification', telling us that God put forward Christ 'as a sacrifice of atonement by his blood' (Romans 3.25). The primary focus here is evil, since suffering, whatever its cause, is evil and not part of God's will. Christ took upon himself not only the suffering of the world but the evil which had caused it. Paul writes that 'in Christ God was reconciling the world to himself' (2 Corinthians 5.19). He took responsibility for the evil in creation and paid the price for it.

The mechanics of how God does this remain a mystery. Nevertheless, hints that the New Testament gives have been worked into 'theories' by theologians down the ages. In the first, the 'Classical Theory', Christ's work is seen as the winning of a cosmic battle between good and evil. The creation is pictured as a territory which has fallen into enemy hands; God is our rightful ruler but he has been usurped by the devil, the present prince of this world. Christ, on the cross, wins it back. A fifth-century bishop put it into words that are still sung:

> Sing, my tongue, the glorious battle,
> Sing the ending of the fray:
> Now above the cross, the trophy,
> Sound the loud triumphant lay:
> Tell how Christ, the world's Redeemer,
> As a victim won the day.

The second theory comes in several different forms, but it is generally referred to as the 'substitution' or 'satisfaction' theory. It has found its way into the consciousness of many English-speaking Christians through the famous hymn 'There is a green hill', and in particular the concluding verse:

> There was no other good enough
> To pay the price of sin;
> He only could unlock the gate
> Of heaven, and let us in.

Essentially, picking up many scriptural references, this theory proposes that Christ stands in our place and has taken all our sins upon his shoulders in order that evil might be dealt with and justice be done.

The third theory, often referred to as the 'exemplarist theory', concentrates attention not so much upon the objective effect of Christ's action on the cross as upon the potential it has to move us to love and goodness. It is expressed poetically in Samuel Crossman's great hymn:

> My song is love unknown,
> My Saviour's love to me
> Love to the loveless shown,
> That they might lovely be.

I have referred to these theories only sketchily since they are limited in their effectiveness: they are all true, but none alone contains the entire truth. This is evident from consideration of such passages as the following:

> And when you were dead in trespasses and the uncircumcision of your flesh, God made you alive together with him, when he forgave us all our trespasses, erasing the record that stood against us with its legal demands. He set this aside, nailing it to the cross. He disarmed the rulers and authorities and made a public example of them, triumphing over them in it. (Colossians 2.13–15)

The first part of this passage speaks of legal demands in terms resonant of the substitution theory, whereas the latter is couched in the terminology of battle with the powers. Other texts in Colossians might be thought of as 'examplarist', exhorting their readers to be as Christ would have them be. For example: 'As you therefore have received Christ Jesus the Lord, continue to live your lives in him, rooted and built up in him and established in the faith, just as you were taught, abounding in thanksgiving' (Colossians 2.6–7). As John de Gruchy, a South African theologian, says of the theories in his magnificent book entitled *Reconciliation*:

> Whatever their explanatory potency in their historical context, their interpretation of scripture and theological reasoning in hindsight often leaves much to be desired. So there is no merit in repeating them as though by doing so we are faithfully representing the Christian doctrine of reconciliation. We

dare not, as W.H. Hodges put it, fall prey to
the tyranny of the theories.[6]

With this in mind, it is instructive to remember
that the Christian creeds are silent about the specific
shape of the atonement. The Church Fathers argued
long and hard about the incarnation and the status
of Jesus as true God and true man, and this is spelt
out in the creeds in great detail. When it comes to
the atonement, we read only that 'he suffered under
Pontius Pilate, was crucified, dead and buried. On
the third day he rose again.' This much is clear: God
is no idle bystander to the world's suffering and nor
is God able or willing to ignore human evil. In his
great love for humankind God in Christ entered the
world and paid the price of evil through his own suffering and death. In the resurrection the triumph of
that love over suffering, evil and death itself is made
manifest. Though we can never understand exactly
how it happened, through Christ 'God was pleased
to reconcile to himself all things, whether on earth or
in heaven, by making peace through the blood of his
cross' (Colossians 1.20). As a result, though suffering
may be a problem both practically and philosophically
for believers, they can believe in Christ's promise to
'make all things new' (Revelation 21.5).

3

Forgiveness and Reconciliation

I want to confess. I do not go to the Catholic
Church, where you can sit in a box and tell
the priest all about the things you have done.
I cannot do that. But I want to talk to somebody,
and that is why I have come to you. (*Kalahari*, 68)

So says Mr Molefelo, who has narrowly escaped with
his life following an armed robbery on his farm, to
Mma Ramotswe. He tells her that he wants to set
things straight so that the next time he faced death
like that he could think that he had set his life in order.
Some church traditions insist upon the necessity of
sacramental confession 'in a box' before sins can be
forgiven; all agree that what is necessary before God's
forgiveness can be felt is repentance. In this instance
the repentance is clear and, as is often the case, the
articulation of it to someone else assists the person
concerned fully to enter into it. That is one of the
reasons why some people find sacramental confession
helpful.

What does Mma Ramotswe do? First, she listens.
She performs a role similar to the priest in the confessional. We are told how shortly after she opened the
No. 1 Ladies' Detective Agency she had discovered
that part of her job would be to listen to people and

to help them unburden themselves of their past. Her hero of private detection, Clovis Andersen, had confirmed this: 'Be gentle. Many of the people who will come to see you are injured in spirit. They need to talk about things that have hurt them, or about things that they have done. Do not sit in judgement on them, but listen. Just listen' (*Kalahari*, 69). Mma Ramotswe does exactly that, displaying again the empathy which seems to come so naturally to her. As she listens to him 'under a sky that had seen so much that one more wicked deed would surely make no difference' she muses that 'sins are darker and more powerful when contemplated within confining walls. Out in the open, under such a sky as this, misdeeds were reduced to their natural proportions – small, mean things that could be faced quite openly, sorted, and folded away' (*Kalahari*, 69).

It is not possible for sins to be 'folded away' until repentance has taken place. Dealing with sin in this manner is necessary because of the pain it causes, not only those who are sinned against but also those who commit sin. Elsewhere in the same novel Mma Ramotswe finds herself (somewhat reluctantly) in a revivalist church meeting. During it 'one man groaned softly, as if in pain, but it was only sin, thought Mma Ramotswe. Sin makes one groan. The weight of sin. Its mark. Its stain' (*Kalahari*, 96). She acknowledges wrong, she acknowledges evil and, unlike many in western society, names it as sin.

Naming sin

The theologian Alistair McFadyen suggests in his book, *Bound to Sin*, that the impotence and public

39

irrelevance of the language of sin is a symptom of what he calls pragmatic atheism: 'our common and collective habits of mind, spirit and agency exclude God from consciousness. We live in our world *as if there were no God* – or at least a God who makes some actual difference to the way in which the world is spoken about, acted in and upon – no matter what personal beliefs or faith we may have.'[1] Mma Ramotswe speaks of wrongdoing as sin and, although the involvement of God is not explicitly mentioned, the fact that the whole episode is couched in the language of sin is implicit recognition of the relevance of God since, as McFadyen explains 'sin is an essentially relational language' which contains 'an inbuilt and at least implicit reference to our relation to God'.[2] The fact that Mr Molefelo, having repented of his sin, wants to confess, is treated by Mma Ramotswe as a very natural and proper thing. She does her best to help him to be relieved of the burden of a sin, committed long ago, 'the weight of which had left a bad mark, a stain'.

She learns how Mr Molefelo, now a respectable civil engineer, had, whilst a student, stolen a radio from the good people with whom he had been lodging in order to fund an abortion for his girlfriend. He feels remorse at having coerced her to have an abortion and at having wronged those who had treated him like a son by having stolen their radio. When he has recounted the whole episode she praises him for his bravery for doing so and adds, 'Most people never tell these stories about themselves. Most people want to make themselves sound better than they are.' Then she asks him simply, 'What do you want to do now?' He explains that he wants her to find the couple so that he can go and confess to them. He wants to make amends for his sin, face what many avoid by confessing it to the person against whom it was committed and, if possible, be reconciled.

Repentance and forgiveness are crucial in themselves but reconciliation should be the ultimate aim of every Christian response to sin, because that is what God has achieved in Christ. Jesus himself talks of the importance of reconciliation in the Sermon on the Mount: 'So when you are offering your gift at the altar, if you remember that your brother or sister has something against you, leave your gift there before the altar and go; first be reconciled to your brother or sister, and then come and offer your gift' (Matthew 5.23–24). Mma Ramotswe recognizes the worth of reconciliation and wants to help him achieve it. She finds the woman, now widowed, and prepares the ground for Mr Molefelo. She explains that he is feeling bad about what he did, has done so for years, and that he wants to come and apologize and buy her a new radio, that he wants to make it up to her. The woman makes clear that she does not want a new radio, at which point Mma Ramotswe asks:

> 'Have you ever done anything wrong yourself, Mma?' Mma Tsolamosese stared at her. 'Everybody has,' she said. 'Yes,' said Mma Ramotswe. 'Everybody has. But do you ever remember wanting to set right some bad thing you have done. Do you remember that at all?' There was a silence between them. Mma Tsolamosese looked away, out across a hillside. Seated on her stool, she was now hugging her knees. When she spoke, her voice was quiet. 'Yes, I do remember that.' Mma Ramotswe lost no time. 'Well, that is

41

how Molefelo feels. And should you not give him the chance to say sorry?' The reply was not immediate, but it did come. 'Yes,' she said. 'It was a long time ago. It is good that he is thinking this now. I would not want him to suffer in his heart.' 'You are right Mma,' said Mma Ramotswe. 'What you are doing is the right thing.' (*Kalahari*, 121)

Mma Ramotswe encourages Mma Tsolamosese to do the good and the right thing by producing in her a sense of empathy. In these books we are encouraged to feel empathy not only with those who have suffered through no fault of their own, but also with those who have done wrong.

Mma Ramotswe then learns that Mma Tsolamosese cares for three grandchildren, and comments that one whose mother has died is 'very pretty and will grow into a very pretty lady in time'. Mma Tsolamosese is upset and explains 'That child ... the mother, who is late, and that disease which has run this way and that through the country, and everywhere. That is what took her. And the child ... the doctor said that the child will become ill too, sooner or later. She will not live. That is why I was upset.' Here again we confront the tragedy of HIV/AIDS through the story of an individual, and are enabled thereby to feel empathy for the huge number of people who suffer from this terrible scourge throughout Africa and in other parts of the world. Mma Ramotswe cannot solve this problem but she does have an idea as to something positive that Molefelo can do which will help him to make amends for his crime. It comes to her as she puts her arm around Mma Tsolamosese and tells her how sorry she is.

To resume the story, Mma Ramotswe arranges for them to meet and Molefelo tells Mma Tsolamosese of his profound regret. Mma Tsolamosese accepts his apology by telling him that a radio is a 'small thing' and that he should not worry. After tea, Mma Ramotswe draws him to one side and says, 'There is a grandchild. There is a little girl. She may not live very long because of this cruel illness. But in the meantime, you could make a difference to that life. You could give Mma Tsolamosese money to use for that child. The right food. Meat. Pretty clothes. Even if the life of that child is short, it would be made a happy one, and if you did that, Rra, then you would have more than made up for what you did all those years ago' (*Kalahari*, 190).

Repentance and forgiveness

By this action Mma Ramotswe enables Mr Molefolo to face his sin and, being penitent, to feel forgiveness in order to 'fold it away'. Further, by finding the girl who had an abortion and arranging for Mr Molefelo to pay for her daughter's passage through nursing school (which enabled him to do something positive without her husband being involved), Mma Ramotswe does something more. Here we see articulated a profoundly Christian way of dealing with sin but also see what many Christians avoid – facing the person who has been wronged and, having been forgiven, doing something positive to make amends. It is not necessary in the Christian scheme of things to do anything to 'pay' for the sin: repentance is all that is required. However, sometimes, the person who has repented wants to do something in order to make clear and celebrate a change of heart. A good example of this is Jesus' encounter with Zacchaeus in which the latter gives away half of all his possessions (Luke 10.1–10). As Timothy Gorringe puts it:

> Forgiveness does not require ... acts of reparation which prove that I am in earnest. On the contrary, forgiveness is prevenient – it enables reparation, expiation, atonement. To attach conditions to forgiveness is to attach conditions to love – but there are no such conditions, for love is free, for nothing.[3]

Forgiveness and reconciliation are very much at the heart of Mma Ramotswe's way with the world. It is not, emphatically not, that she does not judge. 'Of course one could judge others, and Mma Ramotswe used the standards of the old Botswana morality to make these judgements,' we read. She judges but she does not condemn. In western society there is a tendency to confuse judgement and condemnation. There is something important to note here: Christians sometimes succumb to secular pressure that to judge is improper whereas, in fact, it is perfectly proper and necessary to judge. Christians are required to judge between right and wrong: when they do not do so they become woolly. At the same time, having judged, it is necessary to remember that we are not to condemn since to do so will take us along the road towards dangerous fanaticism. To judge but not condemn will require exactly the delicate balance of discernment and empathy we see exhibited by Mma Ramotswe. She uses her considerable powers of discernment to judge but her capacity to empathize enables her to refrain from condemning and, rather, to forgive:

> Mma Ramotswe preferred to forgive, if at all possible. 'I am a forgiving lady,' she said, which was true. She did forgive, even to the extent of bearing no grudge against Note Mokoti, her cruel former husband, who had caused her such grief during their brief, ill-starred marriage. She had forgiven Note, even though she did not see him any more, and would tell him that he was forgiven if he came to her now. Why, she asked herself, why keep a wound open when forgiveness can close it? (*Cupboard*, 5)

Mma Ramotswe gives us a powerful example of what it is to be a forgiving person. Forgiveness lies at the heart of the Christian faith. None of us is perfect. We know that we have sinned and if we are able to recognize that sinfulness in ourselves we should be able to empathize with others and so forgive them, and it is only through the practice of forgiving and being forgiven that there can be any hope for us as individuals or for the world. As we have seen above, Christians believe that 'in Christ God was reconciling the world to himself' (2 Corinthians 5.19). God himself entered into our world in Christ and took upon himself all the sins and pain of the world in order that we might be forgiven; Christians are called to forgive because God has forgiven. More than that, from a Christian perspective we would have to say that we only have the power to forgive because God has already forgiven sinful humanity.

Mma Ramotswe is forgiving and she is merciful. At the beginning of *The Kalahari Typing School for*

Men she is reflecting upon royal personages whom she admires:

> She admired the old King of Swaziland, King Sobhuza II, who had one hundred and forty-one wives, all at the same time. She admired him, in spite of his having all those wives, which, after all, was a very traditional approach to life; she admired him because he loved his people and because he consistently refused to allow the death penalty to be exacted, always – with only one exception in his long reign, a most serious case of witchcraft murder – granting mercy at the last moment. (What sort of man, she wondered, could coldly say to another who was begging for his life: no, you must die?)
> (*Kalahari*, 15)

Christians have long preached the importance of mercy and forgiveness, though they have generally been less good at forgiving. These novels encourage the art of forgiveness. They make clear that in order for true forgiveness to take place and be felt the sin has to be brought to mind and repented of. Forgiveness can lead to reconciliation and both can be encouraged through empathy. It is her empathy with others that enables Mma Ramotswe to forgive, and in the episode recounted above she fosters empathy in Mma Tsolamosese. That empathy enables the latter to exclaim: 'I would not want him to suffer in his heart.' There is a real challenge for Christians here in reflecting upon this link between empathy, and forgiveness and care. 'If you knew what it was like to be another person,' Mma Ramotswe muses, 'then how could you possibly do something which would cause pain?' (*Company*, 7).

Empathy is a central theme of these novels. In *Tears of the Giraffe*, it is empathy with a Mrs Curtain, given her own experience of losing a child, that leads Mma Ramotswe to investigate what happened to Mrs Curtain's son who had disappeared in the bush 10 years previously. It is not pity but empathy that persuades Mr J.L.B. Matekoni to adopt two orphan children. As he sits with Mma Potokwani and contemplates the possibility he 'looked down at his shoes, and remembered, for a moment, how it was to be a child, back in the village, all those years ago. And remembered how he had experienced the kindness of the local mechanic, who had let him polish trucks and help with the mending of punctures, and who by his kindness had revealed and nurtured a vocation. It was easy to make a difference to other people's lives, so easy to change the little room in which people lived their life' (*Tears*, 74). It was this meditation that made him decide to see the children and then offer them a home.

Forgiveness and politics

If forgiveness is possible and appropriate in personal relationships, it is often argued that it can have no place in politics and out there in the 'big bad world'. However, the world has learned from Africa of the political potential of forgiveness, since it was through the practice of forgiveness and the eschewing of retribution that South Africa was able to emerge from the horror of Apartheid. More than anything else, that process was enabled by the extraordinary capacity of Nelson Mandela to forgive. Having been deprived of 27 years of his life, he came out of prison determined to work with those who had deprived him of his freedom, and it was his example and inspiration that enabled others to exhibit a similar, almost superhuman capacity to forgive. In *Tears of the Giraffe* forgiveness is commended by reference to him:

> Then there was Mr Mandela. Everybody knew about Mr Mandela and how he had forgiven those who had imprisoned him. They had taken away years and years of his life simply because he wanted justice. They had set him to work in a quarry and his eyes had been permanently damaged by the rock dust. But, at last, when he had walked out of the prison on that breathless, luminous day, he had said nothing about revenge or retribution. He had said that there were more important things to do than complain about the past, and in time he had shown that he meant this by hundreds of acts of kindness towards those who had treated him so badly. (*Tears*, 55)

Mandela himself wrote: 'In prison my anger towards whites decreased, but my hatred for the system grew. I wanted South Africa to see that I loved even my enemies while I hated the system that turned us against one another.'[4] I well remember seeing a television programme which was charting the first presidential campaign in which he fought following his release. It showed Mandela arriving at a football stadium for an ANC rally. The stadium was packed full of ANC supporters who were baying for the blood of those who had oppressed them so terribly. Mandela stood up in front of them and said, quite simply, 'If I can forgive them, so can you.' From this auspicious beginning was the new South Africa born and, with it, the Truth and Reconciliation Commission which enabled others to emulate Mandela's example. The latter made people do what Mr Molefelo did, face up to and admit their sin. What followed was not punishment and retribution, as might normally be expected in the face of some pretty grim crimes, but, rather, forgiveness and reconciliation.

The importance of the inner life

I have suggested that it is empathy that enables Mma Ramotswe to forgive. What is, it, though, that enables empathy? It is surely the capacity to look fairly and squarely at oneself and be honest with oneself about one's failings as well as one's strengths. One of the main reasons why we do not find it easy to forgive is that we project our own darker side onto others. Nelson Mandela suffered much in prison and it seems to me that during that time he would have had ample opportunity to confront his own 'demons'. Mandela, I would suggest, used his enforced exclusion from 'the world' to achieve the same result as do the best monks by their chosen withdrawal. What they work on during this withdrawal is their inner life. The monk Thomas Merton has some arresting words for those of us who are so concerned about the way the world is. Leaving his monastery for the first time for 12 years he observed:

> I met the world and found it no longer
> so wicked after all. Perhaps the things I

resented about the world when I left it were defects of my own that I had projected upon it. Now, on the contrary, everything stirred me with a deep and mute sense of compassion . . . I seemed to have lost an eye for merely exterior detail and to have discovered, instead, a deep sense of love and pity for the souls that such details never fully reveal. I went through the city, realising for the first time in my life how good are all the people in the world and how much value they have in the sight of God.[5]

Some people never get around to making the connection between their inner life and the feelings which they have about people and places. I had an aunt and uncle who, following retirement, moved 17 times in 20 years. On each occasion they would, after a relatively short time, decide that one of their neighbours was impossible. When I first moved to be a parish priest on inner-city Tyneside a neighbouring parish priest warned me about what he referred to as 'the Wallsend malaise'. He later moved to a beautiful country parish and, mysteriously, the 'malaise' followed him to that place. Our inner life has as much to do with the way in which we perceive and react to people and places as any objective factors about the place itself. The spiritual writer Gerard Hughes points this out in a book he wrote on a pilgrimage he made to the Holy Land. He kept a diary and in it noted those places where he found people friendly on his arrival and those he found unfriendly. When he reflected on his experience, however, he realized that the places he had found friendly were those where he had arrived feeling cheerful and the others those where he had arrived feeling tired and irritable. The places had simply reflected his own mood back to him.

During *In the Company of Cheerful Ladies* Mma Ramotswe tells herself again that 'I'm a forgiving lady.' Her reflection continues:

> I see no point in keeping old arguments alive when it is so simple to lay them to rest. She had made a deliberate attempt to forgive Note, and she thought that it had worked. She remembered the day on which she had done this, when she had gone for a walk in the bush and had looked up at the sky and emptied her heart of its hatred. (*Company*, 125)

If people do not find it 'so simple to lay them to rest' it may be because they have not looked sufficiently at their inner life. Depth psychology speaks of the conflict between consciously held aims and ideals which are at variance with unconscious wishes and fears. The conscious personality is at pains to come to terms with both the world of people and circumstances around it *and* the inner world of largely unconscious fears, desires and impulses. Much conflict in the world arises from the neglect of the inner life: there is surely conflict between nations because there is conflict within nations; there is conflict within nations because there is conflict between people and there is conflict between people, because there is conflict within people. Jesus says that it is 'from within, from the human heart, that evil intentions come: fornication, theft, murder, adultery, avarice, wickedness, deceit, licentiousness, envy, slander, pride, folly. All these evil things come from within, and they defile a person' (Mark 7.21–22). If, on the other hand, we are

able to pay attention to our inner life then the likeli-
hood is that such projection will not occur. What will
emerge instead is empathy with the faults as well as
the sufferings of others, and this will issue in a forgiving person whose first instinct will be to forgive as a
result of having a keen sense of compassion.

Confronting evil

Mma Ramotswe is not naive about the reality of
evil. We are told in *Blue Shoes and Happiness* that
as a young woman she had been too naive to see it in
others:

> The young, Mma Ramotswe thought,
> believe the best of people, or don't imagine
> that people they know, people of their own
> age, can be cruel or worthless. And when
> they find out, and they see what people can
> do, how selfish they can be, how ruthless in
> their dealings, the discovery can be a pain-
> ful one, as it was for her, but it is one that
> has to be made.

In her case it had been through her former husband, Note Mokoti, who had 'transformed her life
from one of happiness and optimism into one of suffering and fear. Such people – men like Note – went
through life spreading unhappiness about them like
weedkiller, killing the flowers, the things that grew in
the lives of others, wilting them with scorn and spite.'
The effect that this had had upon Mma Ramotswe is
instructive:

> Of course it did not mean that one had to
> retreat into cynicism; of course it did not

mean that. Mma Ramotswe had learned to be realistic about people, but that did not mean that one could not see good in most people, however that might be obscured by the bad. If one persisted, if one gave people a chance to show their better nature, and – and this was important – if one was prepared to forgive, then people could show a remarkable ability to change their ways. Except for Note Mokoti, of course. He would never change, even though she had forgiven him, that final time, when he had come to see her and asked her for money and had shown that his heart, in spite of everything, was as hard as ever. (*Blue Shoes*, 157)

She confronts another evil person in *Blue Shoes and Happiness*: as she looked at the face of a blackmailer who was sitting in front of her with its darting, slightly hooded eyes, there was something in the eyes that disturbed her: 'Evil, she thought. That is what I see. Evil. She had seen it only once or twice in her life, and on each occasion she had known it. Most human failings were no more than that – failings – but evil went beyond that' (*Blue Shoes*, 219). Two pages later she asks herself what it is that might have provoked this woman to be so heartless as to blackmail someone: 'And the answer that came back to her was this: hate. Somewhere some wrong had been done, a wrong connected with who she was, perhaps, a wrong which turned her to despair and to hate. And hate had made it possible for her to do all this.' This is an important insight. It is generally true to say that those who perpetrate evil upon others have themselves been hurt, and very often as small children.[6] Research has shown that parents whose behaviour toward their preschool children is responsive, non-punitive, and non-authoritarian have children who show more empathy towards others. The reverse is also true; those who have not been properly loved find it difficult to love and tend to be filled with fear. Love, we read in the first letter of John, casts out fear (1 John 4.18), a thesis put into effect by Mma Potokwani, matron of the 'orphan farm', in her method for dealing with behavioural problems. In her opinion, 'these were almost always due to insecurity and had one cure and one cure alone: love. That, at least, has been her experience, and even if the message was a simple one it was, in her view, utterly true' (*Full Cupboard*, 14). This simple but profound truth that bad behaviour generally comes from insecurity is a crucial one. If one can see that another human being's thoughtlessness or unkindness derives from his or her own hurt, one is more likely to be able to empathize and offer the acceptance and love which will bring healing.

The complications of life

Finding the right way to confront sin is sometimes a complicated matter and we are encouraged at several points during the novels to reflect on this. A case in point occurs in *The Tears of the Giraffe* when Mma Ramotswe and Mma Makutsi are approached by a man who is worried that his wife might be having an affair. Mma Makutsi investigates and ascertains that this is indeed the case but also that the boy whom the client thinks is his son is actually the son of the man with whom she is having an affair: 'His wife has been seeing the same man for many years. He is the husband of a rich woman, who is also a Catholic.

The rich woman does not know about this. The boy is the son of this man and not the client' (*Tears*, 130). This presents them with a moral dilemma not only because telling the man that the boy is not his son would be devastating for him but also because the school fees of the boy, who is bright, are being paid by the rich woman and they do not want him to lose his place at school. Mma Makutsi writes in her report to Mma Ramotswe:

> I do not like to lie, as I am a lady who believes in God. But God sometimes expects us to think about what the results will be of telling somebody something. If we tell the client that the boy is not his son, he will be very sad. It will be like losing a son. Will that make him happier? Would God want him to be unhappy? (*Tears*, 131)

Mma Ramotswe observes that making the right decision in this case is not easy for her, either, since 'as you get older, in fact, you see more sides to a situation' (*Tears*, p. 157). Mma Makutsi responds that the problem they have is very troubling since if they tell the whole truth it will be the end of a very good chance for the boy. The ensuing conversation is worth quoting in full:

> Mma Ramotswe nodded. 'I see that,' she said. 'On the other hand we can't lie to Mr Badule. It is unethical for a detective to lie to the client. You can't do it.'
>
> 'I can understand that,' said Mma Makutsi. 'But there are times, surely, when a lie is a good thing. What if a murderer came to your house and asked you where a certain

person was? And what if you knew where that person was, would it be wrong to say: "I do not know anything about that person. I do not know here he is." Would that not be a lie?'

'Yes. But then you have no duty to tell the truth to that murderer. So you can lie to him. But you do have a duty to tell the truth to your client, or to your spouse, or to the police. That is all different.'

'Why? Surely if it is wrong to lie, then it is always wrong to lie. If people could lie when they though it was the right thing to do, then we could never tell whether they meant it.' Mma Makutsi stopped and pondered for a few moments before continuing. 'One person's idea of what is right may be quite different from another's. If each person can make up his own rule . . .' She shrugged, leaving the consequences unspoken.

'Yes,' said Mma Ramotswe. 'You are right about that. That's the trouble with the world these days. Everyone thinks that they can make their own decisions about what is right and wrong. Everybody thinks that they can forget the old Botswana morality. But they can't.'

'But the real problem here,' said Mma Makutsi, 'is whether we should tell him everything. What if we say: "You are right; your wife is unfaithful"? . . . We are not lying, are we? We are just not telling the whole truth.' (*Tears*, 158)

As she meditated upon this Mma Ramotswe felt that the she was more concerned about the fate of the boy than the adults and that, with this in mind, the best solution would be to tell the truth to Mr Badule but make him accept it so that he would be happy. Mma Makutsi takes up the challenge. She reports to Mma Ramotswe that she has told him that his wife is being unfaithful but that 'he should not do anything about this as his wife was not doing it for herself, but was doing it for her son's sake. She had taken up with a rich man purely to make sure that his son would get a good education. I said that she was being very self-less. I said that it might be best to leave things exactly as they are.' Mma Ramotswe is astounded and asks, incredulously, whether he believed this.

> 'Yes,' said Mma Makutsi. 'he is not a very sophisticated man. He seemed quite pleased.'
>
> 'I'm astonished,' said Mma Ramotswe.
>
> 'Well, there you are, said Mma Makutsi. 'He remains happy, the wife also continues to be happy. The boy gets his education. And the wife's lover and the wife's lover's wife are also happy. It is a good result.'
>
> Mma Ramotswe was not convinced. There was a major ethical flaw in this solution, but to define it exactly would require a great deal more thought and discussion. (*Tears*, 199f.)

McCall Smith does not give us all the answers (as if it were possible to do so) but leaves us with plenty upon which to reflect. What we are given are examples both straightforward and complicated in the life of a woman seeking to lead the good life. She does so very well but she is not, however, uncompromised. Shortly before the above episode she herself had just resorted to blackmail in order to extract information from someone. After the event, she muses:

> As for her own conscience: she had lied to him and she had resorted to blackmail. She had done so in order to obtain information which she otherwise would not have got. But again that troubling issue of means and ends raised its head. Was it right to do the wrong thing to get the right result? Yes, it must be. There were wars which were just wars. Africa had been obliged to fight to liberate itself, and nobody said that it was wrong to use force to achieve that result. Life was messy, and sometimes there was no other way. She had played Dr Ranta at his own game, and had won, just as she had used deception to defeat that cruel witch-doctor in her earlier case. It was regrettable, but necessary in a world that was far from perfect. (*Tears*, 190)

The spectacle of Mma Ramotswe attempting to do the right thing in messy situations is instructive, as is the moral courage she displays in doing so. After she confronts Dr Ranta in *The Tears of the Giraffe* she listened to her own breathing and felt her own heart thumping wildly as she made her way back to the tiny white van. We read that 'She had no idea where she had found the courage, but it had been there, like the water at the bottom of a disused quarry – unfathomably deep' (*Tears*, 172). It has sometimes been argued that courage is not merely a virtue it is *the* virtue in that it requires courage to exercise any of the other virtues so that courage is the expression of virtue.[7] Courage will require self-confidence of a good sort and will best be displayed by those who are secure in themselves in the manner about which I have talked above.

Judgement and forgiveness

Mma Ramotswe has the courage to confront and judge in messy situations – but then she forgives rather than condemns. As she muses to herself after she confronts a Mr Selepeng about his behaviour toward Mma Makutsi, 'I could never be a judge, I could not sit there and punish people after they have begun to feel sorry for what they have done' (*Kalahari*, 183). Despite the cruelty meted out to her she has retained the capacity to be a forgiving person. Because she had looked deep within herself she did not succumb to the temptation to return evil for evil. This is a powerful parable. She could, at the same time, understand the profound connection between being wronged and being tempted, as a result, to do wrong. Mma Potokwani is the same. She confronts the crooked mechanic Mr Mofeli: 'I know you, Herbert Mofeli. I know your mother, she is my friend . . . You were a bad little boy and now you are a bad man, You are just a bully, that's what you are.' She goes on to threaten him that she will tell his mother about him. She later admits to Mma Ramotswe that she does not know his mother and that 'I took a bit of a risk with that. But usually bullies have severe mothers and bad fathers and they are usually frightened of them. That is why they are bullies, I think' (*Morality*, 167–68).

This is further intimation of how important good relationship is from the very start of life. There are those who, when confronted, will, like Note, remain unmoved, but most will respond. Goodness, a giving and forgiving nature like that of Mma Ramotswe, will be infectious just as much as a cheerfulness is: good brings out the good in others, as is demonstrated in these books. They are, as a result, an encouragement in the Christian life.

Mma Ramotswe's ability to strike the correct balance between judgement, empathy and forgiveness is summed up in a passage where she confronts a Mma Tsau, whom, we are told, she had been prepared to dislike.

> But now, in the flesh, with her laboured breathing and her odd walk, it was difficult not to feel sympathy. And of course it was always difficult for Mma Ramotswe not to feel sympathy with another, however objectionable his conduct might be, however flawed his character, simply because she understood, at the most intuitive, profound level what it was to be a human being. Everybody, she felt, could do evil, so easily; could be weak, so easily; could be selfish, so easily. This meant that she could understand – and did – which was not the same thing as condoning – which she did not or taking the view – which she did not – that one should not judge others. Of course one could judge others, and Mma Ramotswe used the standards of the old Botswana morality to make these judgements. But there was nothing in the old Botswana morality which said that

one could not forgive those who were weak; indeed, there was much in the old Botswana morality that was specifically about forgiveness. (*Blue Shoes*, 100)

I have suggested that the suffering she has endured has made Mma Ramotswe compassionate and understanding of the pains and problems of others and the evil into which it sometimes leads them. Her compassion has been formed as well, no doubt, by the fact that she experienced such love, compassion and forgiveness herself from those close to her as a child and a young adult. This is made explicit at the beginning of *The Kalahari Typing School for Men* when Mma Ramotswe muses that, when at last she left Note, she 'would never forget how her father, Obed Ramotswe, whom even today she called the Daddy, had welcomed her back and had said nothing about her husband, not once saying I knew this would happen' (*Kalahari*, 2). In *Morality for Beautiful Girls* we read that

When she had gone to him and told him that Note had left, he had said nothing about her foolishness in marrying him, even if he might have thought about it. He simply said that she must come back to his house, that he would always look after her, and that he hoped that her life would be better now. He had shown such dignity, as he always did. And she had wept, and gone to him and he had told her that she was safe with him and that she need not fear that man again. (*Morality*, 90).

To those familiar with the Christian Scriptures this account will resonate with the story of the Prodigal Son (Luke 15.11–32), which can be said to encapsulate the entire Christian gospel. In it a rebellious son rejects his father's upbringing. Prideful and strong, he insists on receiving his inheritance and heads off to a faraway land, leads a wild life of adventure, and squanders everything of value (literally and symbolically). Not until he is confronted with failure and despair does he return home, repentant and willing to do anything to win back his father's favour. To his surprise, and the surprise of others, he is welcomed, without question, into his father's loving and forgiving arms. No amount of time, no amount of money, and no amount of rebellion could obstruct the father's patient and unconditional love for his son, 'for this son of mine was dead and is alive again; he was lost and is found!' (Luke 15.24). Though he had caused all of his family much pain and loss by his sin, the son is not rebuked by the father but, rather, is feted by him upon his return. The awesome message of this parable is that God is patient and gracious with all of us, yearning to welcome each of us home into loving and forgiving arms. Penitence is necessary to feel the force of that forgiveness, but not for it to be offered.

Forgiveness is the only hope for our world, forgiveness by God and forgiveness of one another. The Christian faith provides us with a philosophical basis for understanding both its functioning and its importance. In this chapter I have tried to show how the novels provide much opportunity to reflect upon this fact.

4

I Call You Friends

> She loved this country, which was a good place,
> and she loved those with whom she lived and
> worked. She had so much love to give – she had
> always felt that – and now there was somebody
> to whom she could give this love and that,
> she knew, was good; for that is what redeems
> us, that is what makes our pains and sorrows
> bearable – this giving of love to others, this
> sharing of the heart. (*Company*, 231).

Christians are called upon to forgive as God has forgiven them and to be reconciled with one another. What next? How might the prodigal son have related to his father and vice-versa *after* his homecoming and forgiveness? There is plenty in these books on which to reflect in considering this question since people and relationships are paramount in the novels, as is made clear in the above passage about Mma Makutsi at the time of her engagement to Mr Phuti Radiphuti.

In *Tears of the Giraffe* Mma Ramotswe meditates briefly upon the shortcomings of Americans and their scientific view of the world:

> The Americans were very clever; they sent
> rockets into space and invented machines

which could think more quickly than any human being alive, but all this cleverness could also make them blind. They did not understand other people. They also thought that everyone looked at things the same way that Americans did but they were wrong. Science was only part of the truth. There were also many others things that made the world what it was, and the Americans often failed to notice these things, although they were there all the time, under their noses. (*Tears*, 100).

At the risk of generalization, whereas western society is heavily task orientated, societies like the one in which these novels are set are, in the main, much more relationship orientated. This came home to me a number of years ago when I used to take groups of young people to Malawi and arranged for them, as part of a link we had with a mission school there, a visit to the homes of students at that school for a weekend. When they returned and I asked them how they had fared, they would be reasonably positive but at the same time puzzled about the fact that they had not actually *done* anything. The most natural thing for an African to do with visitors is just to 'be' with them – sometimes to sit and talk and sometimes just to sit. People in our own society, on the other hand, would generally want to arrange all sorts of activities and outings for visitors coming for the weekend. Such plans are often made in advance, in my experience, without consulting the visitors to find out what they would like to do! The fact is that if one is going to develop empathy with other people then one will need to be able to spend time with them in a relaxed and unhurried setting.

One also needs time to reflect quietly, something which westerners rarely allow themselves to do. The situation is very different in many parts of Africa. We are told that in the No. 1 Ladies' Detective Agency 'there were long hours at the office when nothing very much happened, and these might be spent in conversation, or crocheting, perhaps, or in simply looking up at the ceiling, with its little fly tracks, like miniature paths through the bush' (*Full Cupboard*, 77). We learn that life is even slower in rural areas, like Mochudi, where Mma Ramotswe grew up and where she goes to visit her cousin:

> ... in Mochudi, away from the bustle of Gabarone, Mma Ramotswe could feel herself lapsing again into the rhythms of country life, a life much slower and more reflective than life in town. There was still time and space to think in Gaborone, but it was so much easier here, where one might look out up to the hill and watch the thin wisps of cloud, no more than that, float slowly across the sky; or listen to the cicadas. This was what it meant to live in Botswana; when the rest of the world might work itself into a frenzy of activity, one might still sit, in the space before a house with ochre walls, a mug of bush tea in one's hand, and talk about very small things: headmen in wells, goats and jealousy. (*Full Cupboard*, 31)

Mma Ramotswe hopes to retire to Mochudi, buying some land with her cousins, growing melons, and living life in such a way that

> every morning she could sit in front of her house and sniff at the wood-smoke and look

forward to spending the day talking with her friends. How sorry she felt for white people, who couldn't do any of this, and who were always dashing around and worrying themselves over things that were going to happen anyway. What use was it having all that money if you could never sit still or just watch your cattle eating grass? None, in her view; none at all. (*No. 1*, 162)

Such slowness of living also gives opportunity for people to look inside their own hearts and achieve the sort of integration to which I referred in the last chapter. This will make for better relationships, a theme which is explored in these novels.

Love one another as I have loved you

In his first letter John makes clear the crucial connection between the love of God and the love of our fellow human beings: 'Beloved, let us love one another because love is from God; everyone who loves is born of God and knows God. Whoever does not love does not know God, for God is love'(1 John 4.7–8). He makes the point more bluntly a few verses later: 'We love because he first loved us. Those who say, "I love God", and hate their brothers or sisters, are liars; for those who do not love a brother or sister whom they have seen cannot love God whom they have not seen' (1 John 4.19–20). Jesus himself tells his disciples to 'love one another as I have loved you' (John 15.12). It is not just a request, either, but a command: 'This is my *commandment*, that you love one another as I have loved you.' And how has Jesus loved us? He has loved us as the Father loves him. The passage in

John's Gospel in which this particular commandment appears is known as the Farewell Discourse. It represents, if you like, Jesus' last words to his disciples. This passage is the turning point, the pivot, about which John's Gospel rotates. For, as is made clear in the first letter of John quoted above, God *is* love: it is not just that God approves of love, thinks that it is a good thing, it is not just that God wants us to love one another, commands us to love one another, it is that love is his very essence, he can be no other. 'If you keep my commandments you will abide in my love, just as I have kept my Father's commandments and abide in his love' (John 15.10).

'As the Father has loved me so I have loved you': this is a very profound statement about the nature of God. Divine love, for Christians, is supremely revealed in the incarnation, life, teaching, death and resurrection of Jesus Christ. As well as speaking about the manner in which he has loved us as the Father has loved him, Jesus summarizes the whole of the Jewish law and prophets in the double commandment, that we should love God and our neighbour as ourselves (Mark 12.29–31; Matthew 22.37–39; Luke 10.27). Paul tells us that 'God's love has been poured into our hearts through the Holy Spirit that has been given to us' (Romans 5.5).

What sort of love, though? The countless songs written about love in our society are almost all about a particular sort of love: romantic, sexual love with which western society is obsessed. These novels give a much more balanced view of things and romantic attraction is treated with caution: Precious Ramotswe's disastrous attraction to and marriage to Note Mokoti is hardly a good advert for it. There are frequent references to Mr J.L.B. Matekoni's two young apprentices who shirk from work as much as they can and are besotted with girls, any girls, and, though the main characters are affectionate in their tolerance of them, it is made clear that they are not on a path to happiness. Mma Ramotswe would probably have much sympathy with the worries John Cleese has expressed about the sort of love portrayed in the archetypal 'love stories' which are celebrated in western culture, like *Romeo and Juliet*, *La Traviata*, *Anna Karenina*, *Carmen*, *Anthony and Cleopatra*, *Aida*, *Dr Zhivago*, *Tristan and Isolde*, *Brief Encounter*. As Cleese puts it: 'There's not ten minutes of good, everyday happiness and fun in any of them. The lovers usually get one dollop of over-the-top ecstasy and apart from that it's wall-to-wall suffering. They get stabbed, walled up in tombs, they throw themselves under trains, or commit suicide with asps, they poison themselves or die of consumption or renounce each other in agony.'[1] They are tales of almost unmitigated misery because they idealize a death-dealing kind of love which exults in emotional dependence. *The No. 1 Ladies' Detective Agency* books are somewhat counter-cultural in early twenty-first-century western society in refusing to join the obsession with sex and romantic love which involves dependency.

Christians would do well to turn to the words of Jesus to see exactly what sort of love it is to which he is calling us: 'This is my commandment, that you love one another as I have loved you. No one has greater love than this, to lay down one's life for one's friends. You are my friends if you do what I command you' (John 15.12–14). In this climactic section of John's Gospel Jesus tells us that we are to love one another as he has loved us, and he makes clear that he has loved us by making us his friends. Jesus' disciples are to understand their relationship with him in terms of friendship, 'You are my friends if you do what I command you': Jesus does not offer here a request or a suggestion but an imperative, and the command is to love each other as friends.

The central relationship in these books, alongside the relationship Mma Ramotswe had with her father, is the one she has with Mr J.L.B. Matekoni (we never learn his Christian name), the proprietor of the Tlokweng Road Speedy Motors. Eventually, having known each other for years as friends and after a considerable period of engagement, they are married. It is not true to say that sexual attraction between them is absent. It is rarely referred to, and then only obliquely, as in the following passage concerning a fantasy, 'unconfessed' and 'guiltily enjoyed' in which he helps Mma Ramotswe:

> They were in the Kalahari together and Mma Ramotswe was threatened by a lion. He called out, drawing the lion's attention to him, and the animal turned and snarled. This gave her the chance to escape, while he dispatched the lion with a hunting knife; an innocent enough fantasy, one might have thought, except for one thing: Mma Ramotswe was wearing no clothes. (*Kalahari*, 82)

This brief allusion points to the importance of sexual attraction in any relationship leading to marriage. It cannot, however, be the only thing and if it is accompanied by the sort of emotional dependence characterized by Cleese above it will be disastrous.

The primacy of friendship

For Mr J.L.B. Matekoni and Mma Ramotswe there may well have been sexual attraction from the outset but friendship comes first, it is tested in a long period of engagement before their marriage and it remains thereafter the glue that binds that marriage together. They had been friends long before they were engaged to be married: 'she had taken to dropping in to see him at the garage from time to time, exchanging views about the day's events and enjoying tea which he brewed on an old stove in the corner of his office' (*No. 1*, 83). They were clearly devoted to each other during this period: it would seem that Mma Ramotswe could ask anything of him and he would comply. The reverse would appear to be the case too: a rather reluctant Mr J.L.B. Matekoni is persuaded by another friend of his, the formidable Mma Potokwani, to adopt two children, one of whom is disabled. He agrees without having consulted Mma Ramotswe about the adoption plan, even though she and Mr J.L.B. Matekoni were engaged at the time. It is Mma Ramotswe who, quite uncomplainingly, ends up looking after them (*Kalahari*, 5). She had agreed to marry him 'because she had realised that here was a man who was as good as her father and that they would be happy together' (*Kalahari*, 6). Indeed they were, as a result of a well-founded relationship. After their engagement and marriage it is friendship which is the glue that continues to bind them together. Love is certainly commended in these books, and specifically love within the context of marriage, but friendship even in that relationship is crucial. In a wonderful poem, Mrs Katherine Philips, a friend of the seventeenth-century Anglican divine Jeremy Taylor, referring to friendship as a union, writes:

Nobler than kindred or than marriage-
band
Because more free; wedlock felicity
It self doth onely by this union stand
And turns to friendship or to misery.
Force or design matches to pass may bring
But friendship doth from Love and honour
spring.[2]

If friendship is to be understood as the basic Christian relationship, which I believe it is, then we should expect to find it at the centre of all good relationships, including marriage, as is the case with Mma Ramotswe and Mr J.L.B. Matekoni's. The idea that people should enter into marriage *simply* because they are 'in love', when they are under the influence of what George Bernard Shaw called the most violent, most insane, most delusive, and most transient of passions, is a dangerous one. Friendship, balanced with mature romantic attachment, is a much better basis for a lasting relationship, as in the case of Mma Ramotswe and Mr J.L.B. Matekoni.

Friendship is a relationship which is entered into freely, as Mrs Katherine Philips makes clear in the above poem. It is also, though, something which, unlike marriage and many kinship relationships, is open to all. We are not all called to be mothers or fathers, husbands and wives or brothers and sisters. We can, however, all be friends and it is for this reason that friendship can be held out as the basis for all good human relationships. In another poem sent to a friend, from prison, the great twentieth-century martyr Dietrich Bonhoeffer, who lost his life in defying the scourge of Nazism, makes this very clear:

71

Not from the heavy soil,
Where blood and sex and oath,
Rule in their hallowed might,
Where the earth itself,
Guarding the primal consecrated order,
Avenges wantonness and madness –
Not from the heavy soil of earth,
But from the spirit's choice and free desire,
Needing no oath or legal bond,
Is friend bestowed on friend.[3]

Free the choice might be but, once it has been made, there follows, in true friendship, deep, self-giving commitment. Such commitment will be possible because of the empathy that will have built up between the friends. The root of the word 'empathy' is the Greek word pathos, meaning feeling. People feel for their friends. True friends love one another as did David and Jonathan, 'as their own soul' (1 Samuel 18.1), they love each other 'as they love their own life' (1 Samuel 20.17). They therefore love their neighbours who are their friends as themselves without any difficulty and it is most natural for them to make sacrifices for one another. All true love requires sacrifice, as Paul makes clear in perhaps the greatest of all odes to love ever written, in the thirteenth chapter of his first letter to the Christians at Corinth:

> If I speak in the tongues of mortals and of angels, but do not have love, I am a noisy gong or a clanging cymbal. And if I have prophetic powers, and understand all mysteries and all knowledge, and if I have all faith, so as to remove mountains, but do not have love, I am nothing. If I give away all my possessions, and if I hand over my body so

that I may boast, but do not have love, I gain
nothing. Love is patient; love is kind; love
is not envious or boastful or arrogant or
rude. It does not insist on its own way; it is
not irritable or resentful; it does not rejoice
in wrongdoing, but rejoices in the truth. It
bears all things, believes all things, hopes
all things, endures all things. (1 Corinthians
13)

True friendship is not an abdication of responsibility, a fair-weather relationship. No, love bears all
things and endures all things and will require much
self-sacrifice. It has long been of interest to me that
even a young child understands what is required in
this relationship to which Jesus calls us. Our elder
daughter, presently aged seven, knows exactly what
constitutes true friendship. She has learned from experience that, more than anything else, it demands
loyalty, which may well be costly. Interestingly, Jesus
speaks of various relatives betraying one another:
'they will be divided: father against son and son
against father, mother against daughter and daughter
against mother' (Luke 12.53), but not friends. The
greatest sin in friendship is betrayal – hence Dante
reserved the innermost circle of hell for the notori-
ous betrayers, Judas, Brutus and Cassius. What is,
in one sense, the freest of all relationships, with no
obligations except to delight, to play, carries a hidden
commitment to stay true, stay trustworthy.

Mma Ramotswe gives us an example of such faithfulness and sacrifice in her conduct to her friend Mr
J.L.B. Matekoni before they are married. She nurses
him through his depression and we are given no cause
to think that she at any time wonders whether she

ought to break off her engagement as result of his mental illness. She also shows great patience in waiting for him to name a day. Faithfulness in friendship and faithfulness in marriage are very important to Mma Ramotswe. Sometimes friends will be difficult, and maintaining the relationship will be demanding. This is made clear in the reply Mma Ramotswe gives to Fed-Up Fred on the No. 1 Ladies' Detective Agency website. Fed-up-Fred tells her that he has a friend who is always coming to see him with her problems. He tries to help, but she still keeps complaining and complaining; 'I do not wish to be unkind to her. What shall I do?' Mma Ramotswe responds:

Dear Fed-Up Fred:

Sometimes in Botswana we say that your friends are the people you meet on the path. That means that we must be friends with the people who come into our lives, even if we did not look for them. If we do not like some of these people, we may still have to talk to them and listen to them because they are people like us and they would be sad and unhappy if we ran away when we saw them coming. You must stick by your friend, but what you can do is say to her: Please do not complain all the time because nobody likes to listen to the troubles of others all the time. If this does not work, then you should start complaining to her. Next time you see her, tell her of many sad things that have happened to you. Do not let her say anything, but spend all the time moaning. That may make her think. If that does not work and if you get fed up with moaning, then just talk

74

all the time that she is with you. Talk about all sorts of things, but do not let her get a word in. In this way you will not hear her complaints at all because she will not have the chance to make them.[4]

This would seem to be good improvisation!

Friendship in the Christian tradition

Though Jesus makes clear that friendship is to lie at the heart of human relationship and its worth has been recognized in Christian history, friendship has generally had something of a mixed press. In his autobiographical *Confessions* St Augustine speaks warmly of his experience of friendship before his conversion but then, having been overcome with grief at the death of his closest friend, he becomes quite ambivalent about it, arguing that it is dangerous when an end in itself and not rooted in God and seeking after God. For Augustine, attachment to a friend must be transformed from mutual self-preoccupation to the means by which God draws us to himself. Essentially, for Augustine, friendship should be a school in virtue. Practice in cherishing those whom we love as friends can be an enormous help and inspiration to extend our concern towards others.

In the medieval period great Christian figures like Ambrose of Milan and Anselm of Canterbury commended friendship. Anselm saw the delights of friendship as a foretaste of heaven, an incentive to persevere in the Christian life and a glimpse of its reward. Less well known is Aelred of Rievaulx who writes that a life without friendship is no better than that of a beast, whereas friendship fills one's life with love, affection, security and happiness. He takes it for granted that we are to live in charity with everyone but friendship with only a few: 'We are compelled by the law of charity to receive into the embrace of love not only our friends, but also our enemies. But only those do we call friends to whom we can fearlessly entrust our heart and all its secrets; those, too, who in turn are bound to us by the same law of faith and security.'5 For him, friendship is the highest form of love, which can draw us into the love of God and God's kingdom in the sense that our ultimate destiny is the union of all in God when we all behold each other not as stranger but as friend.

Thomas Aquinas (1225-74), one of the most influential theologians of all time, wrote extensively on friendship, basing his work on the Nicomachean Ethics by the Greek philosopher Aristotle, whose exposition of friendship remains one of the most comprehensive ever undertaken. Thomas Aquinas suggests that life is not complete without it. Life, he argues, has a purpose, the attainment of *eudaimonia*, a Greek word which means something much deeper and richer than happiness. He argued that friendship was to be found within the very heart of God since it was, he held, the friendship love between Father and Son that is Spirit and it is this everlasting community of friendship that we call Trinity. The gift from which love derives is the pouring of God's happiness into our hearts, that divine happiness which is the divine friendship. Further, the gift of God's love to us in Christ allows us to be friends with God as well as with one another.

As the medieval period gave way to the modern another strand in the biblical tradition gradually came to replace this emphasis on friendship as a model for understanding Christian relationship: the one which is symbolized by Jesus saying, 'If any want to become my followers, let them deny themselves, take up their cross daily and follow me' (Luke 9.23). This in turn meant that friendship came to be regarded as less than Christian. It is difficult to say why this change took place since the factors involved, were, no doubt very complicated. Some influential voices, of whose the most vociferous was that of the Danish theologian Søren Kierkegaard (1813-55), suggested that all preferential love like friendship was fundamentally unchristian.

Kierkegaard and those who followed him posited a very strict delineation between the two Greek words *agape* and *philia*, the two Greek words in the New Testament which we might translate love. *Agape* is taken by Kierkegaard to mean a totally self-giving, selfless love characterized by God's love for us in Christ, and *philia*, a weak, self-interested earthly love. This contrast was made most strongly in a very influential book entitled *Agape and Eros* written in the 1930s by a Swedish bishop, Anders Nygren. He argued that *agape* is God's way to humanity: unselfish, giving entirely of itself, whereas *eros* is egocentric self-assertion. *Philia*, which is associated with friendship, is a subset of *eros* since 'egocentric desire is the basis of friendship'. Though the ideas put forward by Nygren have remained influential among Christians, Liz Carmichael, in her book entitled *Friendship*,[6] has pointed out that more recent scholarship suggests that the appearance of *agape* is to be attributed simply to the evolution of the Greek language and not to any theological motivation. Both the verbs *agapan* and *philein* have been shown to have had widely overlapping meanings at the time that the New Testament was written (and Greek has continued to evolve, since *agapan* is the only verb meaning 'to love' in modern Greek and *philein* simply means 'to kiss'). Though the word *agapan* appears more often in the New Testament, 141 times as opposed to 25 for *philein*, the two words are interchangeable. So, for instance, those who 'love' front seats in the synagogue in Luke 11.43 do so with *agapan*, and other first-century writers exchange the two for stylistic reasons.

All this might seem rather esoteric but it is significant since it puts a question mark over whether the New Testament writers wanted to propose a stark contrast between human and divine love in the manner that Kierkegaard and those who have followed him suggest. Other theologians have mused upon the nature of love from a philosophical point of view[7] and have come to the same conclusion: put simply, they question whether we can ever put clear boundaries between selfless love and selfish love. If I go and visit someone in need, it makes me feel better. If I give money to charity, it makes me feel good about myself. In any event, Christians are called to love their neighbour as themselves and if we do not love and care for ourselves then we will not be doing our neighbours any favours if we treat them the same. Charity is what we feel happy to give, not something we want to receive except as a last resort. We all yearn to be liked and not just in receipt of charity. The old saying 'as cold as charity' implies this. Whatever else the love of God is, it is not cold. God yearns for that same warmth to be evidenced in our relationships with one another.

Friendship and civil society

Mma Ramotswe recognizes how crucial faithfulness in marriage and friendship are to the maintenance of a civilized society. Interestingly, in considering the changing morality of modern times, she deals with the two together and suggests that people are now

> far too ready to abandon their husbands and wives because they had tired of them. If you woke up one day and thought that you might find somebody else more exciting than the person you had, then you could just walk out! . . . And friends, too. They could become very demanding, but all you had to do was to walk out. Where had all this come from, she wondered. It was not African, she thought, and it certainly had nothing to do with the old Botswana morality. So it must have come from somewhere else. (*Kalahari*, 116f.)

Such faithfulness will require great self-sacrifice. The trouble is that in abandoning their spouses and friends people will very often be running away from themselves. They will, as a result, take their dysfunction into their next relationship, as turns out to be the case with Mma Ramotswe's first husband, Note.

In Jesus the price of faithfulness in friendship is made explicit: we learn from him that God will never betray us, no matter what the cost, even to suffering and death. 'No one has greater love than this, to lay down one's life for one's friends.' The idea of making sacrifices and even dying for one's friends is not an exclusively Christian ideal. Aristotle can say: 'To a noble man there appears the true saying that he does

79

all things for the sake of his friends . . . and, if need be, he gives his life for them' (Nich.Eth. 1169a), but for Christians this love is given a new significance and meaning: it reveals to us the very heart of God. John tells us in his first letter that those who live in love live in God and God lives in them. That is why Augustine tells us that we know in so far as we love.

Christians have concentrated too much, perhaps, upon Jesus' command to take up our cross and follow him while ignoring the context of friendship in which such sacrificial love is to be placed. If, as Christians, we could rediscover the importance of friendship in our own lives, cherish it and practise it, we would have something of infinite value to offer a world which has lost its moral bearings. I believe that the *No. 1 Ladies' Detective Agency* books have the potential to encourage us in pursuing a virtuous life which has friendship at its centre. However difficult and testing friendship might sometimes be, in these books we see it placed fairly and squarely at the centre of a virtuous life, whereas, as we have seen, in modern times friendship has generally been an underrated thing, both in the Church and in western society. Aristotle extolled what is nowadays quaintly referred to in English as 'civic friendship', the public friendship of people involved in civic life. Nowadays friends in public life are likely to be suspected of nepotism. Friendship should be seen as something positive and good in the public as well as the private sphere, something which can renew the fabric of our society – for true friendship involves vulnerability and mutuality in a manner which banishes the possibility of dominance and oppression. Just think how the world could be transformed if we learned to treat each other as friends. That would restore humanity.

> She loved this country, which was a good place, and she loved those with whom she lived and worked. She had so much love to give – she had always felt that – and now there was somebody to whom she could give this love and that, she knew, was good; for that is what redeems us, that is what makes our pains and sorrows bearable – this giving of love to others, this sharing of the heart. (*Company*, 231)

In the above passage, which I quoted at the beginning of this chapter, McCall Smith is able to make what seems like an easy connection between love of country, love of others in general and the love of an individual in marriage. They all belong together and should feed from one another. In other words, a good marriage should give Mma Makutsi the strength to show love, care and concern for others. However, as we have seen, it is not marriage that is the essential key to this healthy approach to our fellow human beings in general but friendship. These novels give us a good opportunity to reflect upon the fact that not everyone is called to marriage but that all are called to friendship, with God and one another, and that friendship should be a basic constituent of both marriage and the fabric of society. It is friendship which is the link and bond here since it is the basic Christian relationship. In it the Christian faith has something very precious to offer for the renewal of society.

5

To Be the Greatest

Mma Ramotswe believed very strongly that teachers should be treated with respect, as they always had been before the old Botswana morality started to unravel. . . A society that undermined its teachers and their authority only dug away at its own sure foundations. Mma Ramotswe thought this was obvious; the astonishing thing was that many people simply did not understand that this was the case. But there was a great deal that people did not understand and would only learn through bitter experience. In her view, one of these things was the truth of the old African saying that it takes an entire village to raise a child. Of course it does; of course it does. Everybody in a village had a role to play in bringing up a child – and cherishing it – and in return that child would in due course feel responsible for everybody in that village. That is what makes life in society possible. We must love one another and help one another in our daily lives. That was the traditional African way and there was no substitute for it. None. (*Full Cupboard*, 128)

Friendship, I have argued, should be the basis of human relationship but we cannot be friends with everyone. What is needed, as is intimated several places in the books, including the passage above, is corporate responsibility. If such corporate responsibility was 'the traditional African way', it has also been the mainstay of the Judeo-Christian culture on which the foundations of our own society are built. It derives from the biblical witness. Jesus tells his disciples that they must do more than take their share in the responsibility of bringing up children as responsible members of society, they must actually *become* like children. 'Whoever becomes humble like this child is the greatest in the kingdom of heaven' (Matthew 18.4). What on earth does this mean? This godly understanding of greatness is surprising, to say the least. Interpreters have differed as to what characteristic of children was being praised: are we being encouraged to be simple? To be naive? To be trusting? The language of the passage suggests that it was the low station of children in the hierarchy of the family and of society in general at the time of Jesus. But the biblical view of greatness is not just about humility, about not throwing your weight about, as Jesus makes clear later in the Gospel. In Matthew 20.20–28 the mother of the sons of Zebedee ask him to grant them the two foremost places in his kingdom. He answered that, among his disciples, leaders must not seek to lord it over others the way Gentiles leaders did, but that 'whoever wishes to be great among you must be your servant'. So greatness, as God understands it, means becoming like a child in the sense of laying aside status. Only then will people be able to draw alongside one another as 'equals' in order to feel empathy and be one another's true servants.

Getting under the skin of others

This corporate responsibility, as we might expect,
involves teaching children to feel for others, to empathize so that, feeling compassion, they might
learn to serve others. In pondering that some people
were unable to understand what others felt, Mma
Ramotswe reflects:

> The problem was, though, that there seemed
> to be people in whom the imaginative part
> was just missing. It could be that they were
> born that way – with something missing
> from their brains – or it could be that they
> became like that because they were never
> taught by their parents to sympathise with
> others. That was the most likely explana-
> tion, thought Mma Ramotswe. A whole
> generation of people, not just in Africa, but
> everywhere else, had not been taught to feel
> for others because the parents simply had
> not bothered to teach them this. (*Company*,
> 7).

As well as articulating this problem the books are,
as we have seen, an education in empathy themselves.
Service can be encouraged by many means. On
occasions we are given insights into Mma Ramotswe's
thought processes in which she attempts to get 'under
the skin of others'. One such occurs just after the episode in *Morality for Beautiful Girls*, to which I made
reference in Chapter 2, in which Mma Ramotswe
and Mma Makutsi had been reflecting upon the im-
plications of Richard Leakey's anthropological work
in east Africa which suggested that 'we are all from
the same family.' Mma Ramotswe, having recently
promoted Mma Makutsi to become an Assistant

Detective has to break unwelcome news to her about needing to become the secretary of Mr J. L. B. Matekoni's garage. She has already told Mma Ramotswe about the gravity of the financial situation:

> Mma Makutsi was staring at her desk. Then she looked up at Mma Ramotswe and for a moment the branches of the thorn tree outside the window were reflected in her glasses. Mma Ramotswe found this disconcerting; it was as if one were looking at the world as seen by another person. As she thought this, Mma Makutsi moved her head, and Mma Ramotswe saw, for a moment, the reflection of her own red dress.
>
> 'I am doing my best,' said Mma Makutsi quietly. 'I hope that you will give me a chance. I am very happy being an assistant detective here. I do not want to be a secretary for the rest of my life.'
>
> She stopped and looked at Mma Ramotswe. What was it like, thought Mma Ramotswe, to be Mma Makutsi, graduate of the Botswana Secretarial College with ninety-seven per cent in the final examination, but with nobody, except for some people far up away in Bobonong? She knew that Mma Makutsi sent them money, because she had seen her once in the Post Office, buying a postal order for one hundred pula. She imagined that they had been told about the promotion and were proud of the fact that their niece, or whatever she was to them, was doing so well in Gabarone. Whereas the truth was that the niece was

being kept as an act of charity and it was
really Mma Ramotswe who was supporting
the people up in Bobonong.

Her gaze shifted to Mma Makutsi's
desk, and to the still-exposed picture of Dr
Leakey holding the skull. Dr Leakey was
looking out of the photograph, directly at
her. Well Mma Ramotswe? He seemed to be
saying. What about this assistant of yours?
(*Morality*, 12)

As a result of this meditation Mma Ramotswe
tells Mma Makutsi that she will be able to remain
as an Assistant Detective but spend half her time on
secretarial work. This is an example of the manner
in which her empathy works and produces in her a
desire to serve and care for others. In her role as employer, she is clearly the leader but uses her position
of leadership to be of service to her employee so that
together they might be of service to others. The New
Testament has a strong theology of leadership but,
for the Christian, leadership should always be seen
through the lens of service.

We have seen that suffering can produce an empathy
that leads directly to service. In *The Full Cupboard of
Life* we are introduced to the 'House of Hope' which
is a home for 'bad girls' run by a Mr Bobologo. We
learn his reasons for running the home when he tells
Mma Ramotswe that his daughter, his only child, had
run away from home at the age of 16. He eventually
found her in a bar in Mafeking. She did not want to
talk to him and a man had threatened him: 'Go home,
uncle. Your daughter is not your property. Go home,
or pay for one of these girls, like everybody else.' He
had founded the home because 'I said to myself that

I would work to help these girls, because there are other fathers, just like me, who have this awful thing happen to them. These men are my brothers.' He says that he hopes Mma Ramotswe understands that. She swallows before replying: 'I understand very well. I understand. Your heart is broken, Rra. I understand that' (*Full Cupboard*, 154).

Morality and service

In *Morality for Beautiful Girls* Mma Ramotswe meditates on morality:

> Most morality, thought Mma Ramotswe, was about doing the right thing because it has been identified as such by a long process of acceptance and observance. You simply could not create your own morality because your experience would never be enough to do so. What gives you the right to say that you know better than your ancestors? Morality is for everybody, and this means that the views of more than one person are needed to create it. That was what made the modern morality, with its emphasis on individuals and the working out of an individual position, so weak. If you gave people the chance to work out their own morality, then they would work out the version which was easiest for them and which allowed them to do what suited them for as much of the time as possible. That, in Mma Ramotswe's view, was simple selfishness, whatever grand name one gave to it. (*Morality*, 76)

Bishop Trevor Huddleston, an Englishman who devoted most of his life to Africa and who played a major part in bringing Apartheid to an end, used to say that he had been nurtured in ideals of community and service at his Christian school and it was what he had gleaned there that had propelled him into lifelong work for a just and more caring world. One of the great tragedies of our society is that the model of service has been all but lost from view. I am aware of the dangers of romanticizing the past, but was it not common a generation or so ago for people to see their lives in terms of service? Shopkeepers and lawyers, plumbers and doctors, teachers and clergy, bankers and cleaners would all have taken for granted that they did what they did in order to provide a *service* to the community. Moreover, the notion of people being educated to 'serve God, King and country' might seem quaint, at best, but it may have more to commend it that an exclusive interest in 'developing individual potential' to no particular end, which is what is advertised in most current school prospectuses, both independent and maintained, and is what characterizes much of the rationale of education today. What is not entered into is any question of what will bring happiness and fulfilment. A crucial Christian insight is that it is in the service of others that we find fulfilment. Jesus tells us to love our neighbours as ourselves, implying that in loving our neighbours we will be truly loving ourselves. The model of service as a means of understanding life was one of the great contributions of the Christian faith to our society and it has been all but lost from public discourse, as has any notion of vocation. There are many reasons why this has happened, but one crucial one is that our contemporaries find themselves a very long way from the teaching of Christ, who called us to love God and to love our neighbour as ourselves, the implication of the latter of these two great commandments being that it is by loving our neighbour that we can best love ourselves with a proper love, a love that will bring fulfilment and meaning. That the same is happening in Africa is implied in the books; Mma Ramotswe muses that the Ten Commandments gave a perfectly good set of guidelines for the conduct of one's life:

> Everybody knew that it was particularly wrong to kill, everybody knew that it was wrong to steal; everybody knew that it was wrong to commit adultery and to covet one's neighbour's goods . . . She hesitated. No they did not. They did not know that at all, or at least, not any more. There were children, horrible cheeky children being brought up with precisely the opposite message ringing in their ears, and that was the problem, she thought grimly. (*Kalahari*, 116)

The problems which have long afflicted the West are beginning to grip parts of Africa. Societies which once put relationships first are being changed, and not exclusively for the better. As Mma Ramotswe puts it:

> It was all very well being a modern society, but the advent of prosperity was a poisoned cup from which one should drink with the greatest caution. One might have all the things which the modern world offered, but what was the use of these if they destroyed all that which gave you strength and courage and pride in yourself and your country?

Mma Ramotswe was horrified to read of
people being described in the newspapers
as consumers, That was a horrible, horrible
word, which sounded rather too like
cucumber, a vegetable for which she had
little time. People were not just greedy
consumers, grabbing everything that came
their way, nor were they cucumbers, for
that matter, they were *Batswana*, they were
people! (*Company*, 161)

Inspired to serve

The theme of service is one that is referred to often
in the books. Mma Ramotswe's models in this are
Seretse Khama, first President of Botswana, and
Queen Elizabeth II. As she says of a meeting between
the two: ' . . . when Queen Elizabeth II met Seretse
Khama she knew immediately what sort of a man he
was. She knew because she could tell that he was the
same sort of person as she was: a person who had been
brought up to serve' (*Kalahari*, 15). Queen Elizabeth
'had been on duty for fifty years, Mma Ramotswe
said, just like Mr Mandela, who had given his whole
life for justice' (*Full Cupboard*, 190). She reflects elsewhere that she would have been very sad to lose her
Queen Elizabeth II teacup 'because it reminded her
of duty and of the traditional values in a world that
seemed to have less and less time for such things. Not
once had Seretse Khama faltered in his duty, nor had
the Queen' (*Company*, 13).

The Queen is inspired by her Christian faith and
has spoken of that faith more readily in recent times.
She is inspired by Jesus who, on the night before he

was betrayed, gave the most memorable demonstration of the importance of service when he washed his disciples' feet and told them that they were to do likewise. It is in service and in that alone, that we can find the fulfilment we crave – and as we do so enable a just and equitable, caring and responsible society. Mma Ramotswe looks to the example of Queen Elizabeth II and Seretse Khama for her inspiration. Millions of people have been and are inspired by the latter two. It is not only people like the Queen and Seretse Khama who can inspire others to serve: fictional characters like Mma Ramotswe can likewise encourage through the narrative of these books.

Archbishop Desmond Tutu said once that 'an enemy is a friend waiting to be made; that is the only hope for this conflict ridden world'. Jesus himself says as much when he tells us that we are to love our enemies: 'You have heard that it was said, "You shall love your neighbour and hate your enemy." But I say to you, Love your enemies and pray for those who persecute you, so that you may be children of your Father in heaven, for he makes his sun rise on the evil and the good, and sends rain on the righteous and the unrighteous' (Matthew 5.43–45). The Christian vision of what the world should look like is an inspiring but a daunting one. It is clear that not everyone whom we come across will behave as we would want friends to behave. Not everyone will act according to what is known as the 'golden rule' in religion, that we should treat others as we would want them to treat us. By attempting to be honest about ourselves, by having empathy for others, by letting that empathy develop into compassion and the capacity to forgive, by responding to Jesus' call to make friendship the basis for our relationships, we are more likely to be able to treat well those who abuse us, as Mma Ramotswe does Note. The conclusion of her final encounter with him, when he has tried to blackmail her, reads as follows:

> Note looked at her, a look of pure hate, and for a moment Mma Ramotswe was afraid again, but then she stopped herself and taking a deep breath, she stepped towards him. Now they were face to face, and when she spoke she did not have to speak loudly. 'I loved you,' she said, making sure that he should hear each word. 'You were not good to me. Now that is all over. I do not hate you, Note Mokoti, and I am . . .' – she paused. It was hard to say this, but she knew that she had to. 'I want you to go in peace. That is all.' And she spoke in Setswana those two simple words that mean Go in peace, Go slowly.
>
> Then she reached into the pocket of her skirt and took out a small envelope. Inside there was some money – not ten thousand pula by any means, but some money to help him.
>
> 'I do not hate you, ' she repeated.' 'This is a gift from me. It is to help you. Please go now.'
>
> Note looked at the envelope which was being held out to him. For a moment he hesitated, but then he reached forward and took it. He looked at her. 'Thank you,' he said, and then he turned and began to walk away. (*Company*, 214)

Most of the acts of kindness and goodness that we are called to will be less dramatic, less spectacular, than was this one for Mma Ramotswe. But it was a lifetime of schooling in these lesser acts that gave her the strength and inspiration to do this extraordinary thing to Note. As she observes 'Sometimes we are able to do something that helps somebody else. That's the important thing. That makes our job a good one' (*Company*, 69). That is what she did, day in and day out, improvise on the good life as it is given to us in the Christian faith. Some of the many episodes in which we learn of something good being done are charmingly down-to-earth. For example, having been offered a lift home by a man who was not exactly the one she had imagined meeting at a dancing class Mma Makutsi wonders whether to accept. She looked at him and

> noticed that there were dark brown patches in the armpits of his shirt. We are all human, all creatures of water and salt, all human. And she thought for a moment of her brother, her poor brother Richard, whom she had loved and looked after, and who had suffered from those dreadful fevers that bathed him in sweat at night. She could not hurt this man; she could not say to him, no, I cannot accept your kindness. (*Company*, 91)

This simple act of mercy and kindness on Mma Makutsi's part began a relationship which led to her marriage.

In looking at the manner in which these novels encourage service, we have been able in this chapter to engage with the fact that the Christian life is best seen in terms of service and to be reminded that the model of service is one of the most precious things that the Christian faith has given to western society, unfashionable though it now is as a way of understanding what life is and should be. Serving one another lovingly is, in fact the only thing of any worth that we have to give as human beings, as is beautifully expressed in Susan Wood's poem, 'A Dusty Mirror'. Susan Wood, who died in 2006, was born in Africa of English missionary parents and spent almost all her life there, serving Africans.

> I would give you
> The golden ball of the world
> The glittering canopy of space,
> If these would be your cure
> And in my power to give.
>
> But for your need
> I offer all I have.
> What have I for your comfort
> But this poor human cloak
> Spread for you
> Lovingly?

6

Here and Hereafter

The nurse looked at Mma Makutsi and gestured
for her to sit on the floor beside them. Then,
still holding his hand, she reached forward and
gently touched his cheek. 'Lord Jesus,' she said,
'who helps us in our suffering. Look down on
this poor man and have mercy on him. Make
his days joyful. Make him happy for his good
sister here who looks after him in his illness.
And bring him peace in his heart.' Mma Makutsi
closed her eyes, and put her hand on the
shoulder of the nurse, where it rested, as they sat
in silence. (*Morality*, 36)

So prays the nurse from the Anglican hospice when
she comes to see Richard, Mma Makutsi's brother,
for whom Mma Makutsi is caring as he dies from
AIDS. It could be thought strange that we have got
this far in a book on theology without there having
been much mention of prayer and worship which, for
Christians, are central not only to the exercise of the
good life but to its sustenance. Living love requires
acknowledgement of and relationship with God who
is Living Love and who can enable us to live in love
by the power of the Holy Spirit. Prayer and worship
feature in the books but, like all the most important
aspects of Mma Ramotswe's life – her relationship to

her father and her husband, the loss of her child – are understated. Behind the statement that, like half of Botswana, she 'thought the church way' lies a great deal, though explicit references, like the one above, are few.

In this reference it is suggested that God is able to come to the aid of those who are suffering. Whereas most of what has been talked about in this book – the overcoming of suffering through good, the importance of forgiveness and reconciliation, the potential of friendship, the model of service – could be readily understood by believers and non-believers alike, at this point there is a radical divergence. Talk of sin, as we have seen in Chapter 3, requires an implicit acknowledgement of God in a society which has become pragmatically atheist. Here the existence and activity of God is made explicit. Recourse to God in prayer and the accompanying expectation of intervention is assumed here in an unselfconscious manner. It is highly counter-cultural.

The importance of prayer

Most Christians would accept that intercessory prayer is intrinsic to a good and godly life but would become somewhat embarrassed if asked to talk about it in an increasingly secular world. The New Testament speaks much of healing and prayer for those who are sick and it is specifically commended in the letter of James:

> Are any among you sick? They should call on the elders of the church and have them pray over them, anointing them with oil in the name of the Lord. The prayer of faith will

save the sick, and the Lord will raise them up; and anyone who has committed sins will be forgiven. Therefore confess your sins to one another, and pray for one another, so that you may be healed. The prayer of the righteous is powerful and effective. (James 5.14–16)

In these books it is generally taken for granted, in a manner increasingly rare in western Europe but quite natural in other parts of the world, that prayer is just a part of life, that praying for people is a sensible and practical manner in which to help them. One of the great gifts given to the Christian is the possibility, through intercessory prayer, of helping someone who is in need when all earthly methods have been exhausted. Intercessory prayer is of benefit to the person who is praying, as well. It gives an opportunity to 'be with' that person before God and, in so doing, both to develop empathy with that person, a quality we have seen to be of huge importance in the good life, and at the same time to align oneself with the loving purposes of God who is Living Love.

This latter point reminds us that prayer is about more than asking for things. Prayer is a living growing relationship with God. We have seen how the inspiration and example of others are crucial in the leading of the good life. For the Christian, who understands God to be the supreme Good, it is necessary to be in a developing relationship with God in order to proceed in the good life. Prayer should enter into every aspect of our lives as is suggested in these books. In *The Full Cupboard of Life* we read, 'Then she said grace, as she always did, her eyes lowered to the tablecloth, as was proper' (*Full Cupboard*, 105).

On other occasions grace before meals with Mr J.L.B. Matekoni and the children is mentioned in a manner that makes it clear that grace was as much a part of the meal as eating and drinking. The saying of grace is something which has almost disappeared from most households in western Europe, even Christian ones. This is a real loss because grace serves as a powerful reminder that the many good things we have are gifts, gifts from God. We need to remind ourselves that God's purposes are loving and good, and that if we will have eyes to see we will be able to discern that fact. Thankfulness should be the basic Christian attitude in prayer as in life: the Prayer Book Communion Service tells us that 'it is meet and right at all times and in all places to give thee thanks and praise' and grace helps to remind us of this on a regular and frequent basis. Saying grace is part of the discipline of 'counting one's blessings' which Mma Ramotswe had learned to do at an early age:

> Oh yes, God had given a great deal to Botswana, as she had been told all those years ago at Sunday school in Mochudi. 'Write a list of Botswana's heavenly blessings,' the teacher had said. And the young Mma Ramotswe, chewing on the end of her indelible pencil, and feeling the sun bearing down on the tin roof of the Sunday school, heat so insistent that the tin creaked in protest against its restraining bolts, had written: (1) the land; (2) the people who live on the land; (3) the animals, and specially the fat cattle. She had stopped at that, but, after a pause, had added: (4) the railway line from Lobatse to Francistown. This list, once submitted for approval, had come back with a

> large blue tick after each item, and the comment written in: Well done, Precious! You are a sensible girl. You have correctly shown why Botswana is a fortunate country. (*Full Cupboard*, 1)

Like many Christian disciplines, counting one's blessings is to be recommended not only because it is the right thing to do but because it will make those who do so happier. Reflecting upon and giving thanks for our blessings – including food – will help to remind us how fortunate we are. It is a feature of our fallen human nature often to concentrate our attention upon the things in our lives which are unsatisfactory. The discipline of counting one's blessings might nowadays be known as cognitive therapy but, as is the case with so many profound psychological insights, what amounts to cognitive therapy is to be found in the Christian gospel. I proposed in Chapter 3 that it is vital for us to work on our inner lives in order to proceed in the good life, and the developing of an attitude of thankfulness is one way in which this can be done. The fact that the delightful list of blessings enumerated by Mma Ramotswe does not contain ones that might generally be thought to be the essential ingredients of a fortunate life should not be dismissed simply as the consequence of her being a child. We all need to think rather more laterally than we generally do about the blessings of this life and the above list is an encouragement to do so. The regular saying of grace also reminds us that prayer should be as matter-of-fact and normal a part of life as eating and drinking and sleeping.

When we read in the novels of Mma Ramotswe attending worship on a Sunday, the implication is that

this is what she normally did. By attending church
she would be put in touch again with the Christian
Scriptures which have formed her and inform her life;
she would be given the opportunity to reflect upon
them anew and seek God's grace in helping her to live
by them; she would be able to receive the living Lord
sacramentally under the forms of bread and wine and
so receive his strength and his grace; she would be
able to give thanks formally for the blessings that God
had showered upon her and seek his help with the difficulties that faced her; she would be able to pray for
others as well as herself; she would be surrounded by
others of faith and encouraged in a common calling
which relates to Living Love and seeks to bring love
into the world.

An eternal perspective

In attending church Mma Ramotswe would also,
perhaps most importantly, be encouraged to see her
life in an eternal perspective. Reference is made to
this eternal perspective when Sister Banjule, the nurse
from the Anglican hospice, attends to Mma Makutsi's
brother Richard after he has died:

> And then the neighbour, who had been
> standing near the door, led Mma Makutsi
> away so that Sister Banjule could ensure in
> private the last dignities for a man whose life
> had not amounted to very much, but who
> now received, as of right, the unconditional
> love of one who knew how to give just that.
> *Receive the soul of our brother, Richard,*
> said Sister Banjule as she gently took from
> the body its stained and threadbare shirt

and replaced it with a garment of white,
that a poor man might leave this world in
cleanliness and light. (*Full Cupboard*, 75)

This passage speaks of human dignity and, movingly, of the 'unconditional love' of God which is reflected in the ministry of his servant, Sister Banjule. That unconditional love is not something that evaporates at death and it is for that reason that Mma Makutsi's brother's body is treated with great dignity. Paul teaches us that our bodies are the temple of the Holy Spirit and this is recognized and affirmed by Sister Banjule.

Mma Ramotswe herself refers to what might happen beyond death in a memorable scene in *Blue Shoes and Happiness* where she is asked to pose in a photograph with an American tourist. Afterwards, the tourist's travelling companion who took the photograph thanks her and confides that her friend is very ill and that, though they have travelled to many places together, this is their last trip. The narrative continues:

For a moment Mma Ramotswe stood quite still. Then she turned and walked back to the table, to stand beside the woman, who looked up at her in surprise. Mma Ramotswe went down on her haunches, squatting beside the thin woman, and slipped her arm around her shoulder. It was bony beneath the thin blouse, and she was gentle, but she hugged her, carefully, as one might hug a child. The woman reached for her hand, and clasped it briefly in her own, and pressed it, and Mma Ramotswe whispered very quietly, but loudly enough for the woman to hear, *The*

Lord will look after you, my sister, and then
she stood up and said goodbye, in Setswana,
because that is the language that her heart
spoke, and walked off, her face turned away
now, so that they should not see her tears.
(*Blue Shoes*, 131)

Here we see Mma Ramotswe's great empathy
extending its reach to someone whom, though she
was a complete stranger and a foreigner, she felt for
acutely. It is a moving example of cross-cultural empathy: whilst AIDS is the scourge of Botswana it is
cancer that more westerners fear. Mma Ramotswe's
empathy gave her not only the will to say something
but the right words to say: 'The Lord will look after
you' is perhaps the best thing that can be said by a
person of faith to another who is dying. It is assumed
in this passage and in Mma Ramotswe's words of
assurance that all of us, as human beings, are made
to be in relationship with God, that the God of love
who created us cares for us and that this relationship
of care continues beyond death. Mma Ramotswe's
words speak of the eternal perspective in which
Christians are called to lead their lives as a result.
Mma Ramotswe muses on this perspective for herself
in *Blue Shoes and Happiness*:

She thought of her father, the Daddy as she
called him, every day. And when she thought
of those dreams at night, he was there, as
if he had never died, although she knew,
even in the dream, that he had. One day she
would join him, she knew, whatever people
said about how we came to an end when we
took our last breath. Some people mocked
you if you said that you joined others when

your time came. Well, they could laugh, those clever people, but we surely had to have hope, and a life without hope of any sort would be no life: it was a sky without stars, a landscape of sorrow and emptiness. If she thought that she would never again see Obed Ramotswe, then it would make her shiver with loneliness. As it was, the thought that he was watching her gave a texture and continuity to her life. And there was somebody else she would see one day, she hoped – her baby who had died, that small child with its fingers that had grasped so tightly around hers, whose breathing was so quiet, like the sound of the breeze in the acacia trees on an almost-still day, a tiny sound. She knew that her baby was with the late children in whatever place it was that the late children went, somewhere over there, beyond the Kalahari, where the gentle white cattle allowed the children to ride upon their back. And when the late mothers came, the children would flock to them and they would take them in their arms. That was what she hoped, and it was a hope worth having, she felt. (*Blue Shoes*, 117)

The Christian hope

The point that is reinforced by this meditation is that belief in the afterlife is crucial. Paul remonstrates with the Christians at Corinth that: 'if Christ is proclaimed as raised from the dead, how can some of you say that there is no resurrection of the dead? . . . If for this life only we have hoped in Christ, we are of all people most to be pitied' (1 Corinthians 15.12, 19). Belief in resurrection is pivotal to the Christian faith and, contrary to what is sometimes suggested, the notion is intellectually defensible. In a substantial tome on the subject, entitled *The Resurrection of the Son of God*, Tom Wright presents a closely argued and meticulously researched argument to the effect that the empty tomb and the 'meetings' with Jesus, when combined, present us with 'not only a sufficient condition for the rise of early Christian belief but also, it seems, a necessary one. Nothing else that historians have come up with has the power to explain the phenomena before us.'[1] It is belief in the resurrection of Jesus which allows belief in the general resurrection and, as is implied by Mma Ramotswe's meditation, such belief is important in the here and now. If we see our lives in an eternal perspective we shall lead them differently and better in the present because they will be of hugely more significance. Christian hope helps to give us the courage to confront the struggles, temptations and pain of the world.

The resurrection is important for another reason, as is articulated by John Polkinghorne, who recounts the story of the Sadducees' attempt to catch Jesus out with the conundrum about a woman who had been married to a succession of brothers, and Jesus' comment concerning God as the God of Abraham, Isaac and Jacob. Jesus responds to them that God is 'God not of the dead but of the living'. Polkinghorne tells us that the point of the story is as follows: 'If Abraham, Isaac and Jacob mattered to God once – and they certainly did – they matter to him for ever. The same is true of you and me. God does not just cast us off as discarded broken pots, thrown onto the rubbish heap of the universe when we die. Our belief in a destiny beyond death rests in the faithful-ness of the eternal God.'[2] Polkinghorne goes on to ask whether this makes sense. He rejects a dualistic notion of soul and body and suggests, in accordance with Hebrew thinking and modern insights, that we appear to be animated bodies rather than embodied souls.[3] Observing that the material of our bodies is changing all the time and that there are very few atoms of our bodies left from among those that were there a few years ago since, 'eating and drinking, wear and tear, mean that they're continually being replaced', he suggests:

> The real me is an immensely complicated 'pattern' in which these ever-changing atoms are organised. It seems to me to be an intelligible and coherent hope that God will remember the pattern that is me and recreate it in a new environment of his choosing, by his great act of resurrection. Christian belief in a destiny beyond death has always centred on resurrection, not sur-vival. Christ's Resurrection is the foretaste and guarantee, within history, of our resur-rection, which awaits us beyond history.[4]

Polkinghorne reminds us that we are talking of resurrection into a new world and that this is dif-ferent from resuscitation into the old one since the Scriptures talk of a new heaven and a new earth. It is, he tells us, the pattern that signifies, not the matter that makes it up but he is clear that this new 'world' will be a material one. This is not a 'pie in the sky when you die' approach. Mma Ramotswe's hope in a resurrected Botswana is not an entirely fanciful one, it is a substantial one. The Christian Scriptures speak in different but resonant tones:

> And I heard a loud voice from the throne saying 'See, the home of God is among mortals. He will dwell with them; they will be his peoples, and God himself will be with them; he will wipe away every tear from their eyes. Death will be no more; mourning and crying and pain will be no more, for the first things have passed away.' (Revelation 21.3–4)

She is right to feel that 'a life without hope of any sort would be no life', 'a sky without stars, a landscape of sorrow and emptiness'. Equally importantly, Mma Ramotswe is right to suggest that this hope 'gives texture and continuity' in the present. It matters and has an effect in the here and now. She knows in her heart that she matters, matters eternally, and so do all the things and people whom she loves. This hope will be of huge significance in encouraging her in the good life because she wants to make it clear to others that they matter and what they do matters. Further, she can work for the good in the here and now with confidence because she has hope and faith that, in God's providence, good will triumph. Paul, in 1 Corinthians 13, links together faith and hope and love. This is surely because it is Love, the living love of God, that begets faith and hope and it is then faith and hope that issue in loving lives. 'And now faith, hope and love abide, these three, but the greatest of these all is love' (1 Corinthians 13.13). This is because it is love, living love, that is the beginning and end of all things.

Alexander McCall Smith has published a book
of sermons preached by his friend Trevor Mwamba,
Bishop of Botswana, who appears as a character in
the novels. It is entitled *Dancing Sermons* and the
first one was preached in the Cathedral of the Holy
Cross, Gaborone, on Easter Day 2005. Bishop Trevor
says:

> We live in a wonderful and miraculous
> world. This, in effect, is what Easter is
> about. It is pulling the curtains apart to
> reveal a world of wonder, of miracles. It is the
> realization that God is always doing these
> miracles especially when we suffer. When
> bad things happen to us. When things don't
> make sense, when we give up in the face of
> problems. Easter is the realization that God
> is always at the centre of things, transform-
> ing bad situations into good. The realization
> that God is greater than we think and there
> is more to life than we imagine. Much more.
> On that first Easter many centuries ago this
> is what the disciples realized. This is what
> we must realize every day of our lives: the
> transforming Easter magic of God still
> touches us now.[5]

These words make the crucial connection between
resurrection and our life in the here and now. They
bid us remember that 'God is always at the centre of
things transforming bad things into good' and therefore that we, like Mma Ramotswe, should dedicate
our lives to being part of God's purpose that good
should prevail. Such words should help us, too, help
us to be filled with joy as we do so.

Christian joy

From the beginning the resurrection has brought joy. We read in Luke's Gospel: 'And they worshipped him and returned to Jerusalem with great joy' (Luke 24.52). There are only two resurrection appearances in Luke and in this final one, as in the first on the road to Emmaus, Jesus appears to the disciples and 'opens their minds to understand the scriptures to them' (24.45). In the former passage, (24.27) he interprets to them in all the scriptures the things concerning himself, beginning with Moses and the prophets. In this one, he makes clear to them from the scriptures how it was written that the Christ should suffer and on the third day rise from the dead. And what is the reaction of the disciples? Joy, just as the hearts of the two disciples on the road to Emmaus burned with joy as he opened the scriptures to them.

Christ came to bring joy: he speaks to his disciples of God's great love for them' so that their joy may be complete'. It permeates all that he says and does. Joy is the hallmark of the resurrection appearances in Luke. The joy of the disciples of which we read at the conclusion of Luke's Gospel became a hallmark of the Christian life when the Holy Spirit fell upon the disciples. Joy is one of the fruits of the Spirit. We learn in Acts 13.52 that the disciples were filled with joy and the Holy Spirit. Paul tells the Romans that the kingdom of heaven is righteousness and peace and joy in the Holy Spirit and prays that they may be filled with all joy and hope in believing. Mma Ramotswe is able to show joy in her life. When she prepares her accounts for the end of the financial year, she finds that:

she had not made a lot of money, but she had
not made a loss, and she had been happy
and entertained. That counted for infinitely
more than a vigorously healthy balance
sheet. In fact, she thought, annual accounts
should include an item specifically headed
Happiness, alongside expenses and receipts
and the like. That figure in her accounts
would be a very large one, she thought.
(*Tears*, 200)

Happiness is not the same as joy but the sort of
continuing deep-down happiness referred to here is
very close to it. Sometimes we shall be weighed
down by burdens and by evil and we should not
underestimate its power. However, it should not sully
our joy because, as Paul emphasizes to the Romans,
'neither death nor life, nor angels, nor rulers, nor
things present, nor things to come, nor powers, nor
height, nor depth, nor anything else in all creation,
will be able to separate us from the love of God in
Christ Jesus our Lord' (Romans 8.38–39). That
knowledge can carry us through the darkest of times
in life and ministry. Archbishop Desmond Tutu is
someone full of joy and laughter and I interpret this
as a sign that he has been able to keep a godly perspective on things, rather than be weighed down
with the terrible situations which he has had to confront.

The conviction that God's love has triumphed
over all that is evil and over death itself gives a
sound basis for joy in this life, since God calls us
to friendship not just now but into all eternity.
Christians tend to be rather tacit about the
resurrection in modern western society. They need

to be more confident in expressing its truth and its power.

7

The Divine Drama

The title of this series is 'Conversations'. In this book
I have attempted a conversation between the *No. 1
Ladies' Detective Agency* series and the Christian
faith, about which it has much to say, both explicitly
and implicitly. I have entitled the book *Living Love*
since I believe that this conversation can throw light
both upon God, who is Living Love, and upon the
way in which we are called to live lives of love. This is
a practical book which seeks to extol and to encourage the good and godly life.

In the past few years, philosophers who reflect upon
ethics (of whom Alexander McCall Smith is one) have
commended what they refer to as 'virtue ethics', as
opposed to 'quandary ethics'. Quandary ethics, which
is what most of us have been encouraged to think
ethics is all about, concentrates attention upon what
one would do if faced with a difficult decision, like,
for example, when a mother is dying and a choice
has to be made between her life and that of her child.
Virtue ethics is more interested in decisions about
which we do not even have to stop to think. If I ask
someone why he or she went to the help of the victim
of a car accident the answer would quite probably be
'Well, that's just what you do, isn't it?' The reason
why people are able to make such a response is that
they have lived in a society in which helping people in

such situations is taken for granted. Virtue ethicists speak, after Aristotle, of the importance of forming 'communities of virtue' in which people can encourage one another in the good life.

The fact that people respond to the needs of others without thinking is not, in fact, 'just what you do'. It is, rather, a result of being part of a society in which the Christian ethic has been part of our mental furniture for hundreds of years. There is nothing to suggest that helping people is 'natural'. That is not to say that there are not religious traditions other than the Christian one that support such an approach – there are. It is simply to clarify that in western society our life has been shaped by that particular ethic. Generations of people have taken to heart the story of the Good Samaritan and its moral has become embedded deep within our culture. It is seen in the lives of individuals and in some of our best institutions, one of which is the National Health Service. Behind the formation of the latter lies the conviction that sickness and accidents which are suffered by individuals should be responded to collectively and caringly, a conviction rooted in and nurtured by the Christian faith. The NHS is an example of an institutional response to the question asked of Jesus in the story of the Good Samaritan, 'And who is my neighbour?'

If this has been true for a very long time there is reason to fear that it is no longer so and that, as a result, society in western Europe is living on borrowed time. The majority of the population is very much less familiar with the Christian Scriptures than has been the case in the past. Most people, for instance, would now find it odd to suggest that there is any significant link between the National Health Service and the Christian faith. If it is the Judeo-Christian ethic that has had a large part in promoting and sustaining virtue in the West, our contact with that ethic is becoming more and more tenuous and so one of the prime well-springs of our most basic values is being cut off. Mma Ramotswe herself articulates the difficulty:

> The problem, of course, was that people did not seem to understand the difference between right and wrong. They needed to be reminded about this, because if you left them to work it out for themselves they would never bother. They would just find out what was best for them and call that the right thing. (*No.1*, 33)

I have tried to show how engaging with these books takes us back to our roots and, both directly and indirectly, makes connections between the Christian faith and the good life. The books serve to remind us of the difference between right and wrong and encourage us in choosing the right. Mma Ramotswe provides us with a good and inspiring example of how Christian formation through immersion in the Scriptures and the life of the church can issue in a life in which the loving course of action comes naturally. If Christian life is sustained, as is Mma Ramotswe's, through prayer and worship, there is then a sense in which the rest should follow almost unconsciously. There is an analogy here with the way in which McCall Smith writes the books in the series. At the beginning of this book I mentioned how the inspiration for them had come from him seeing a woman chasing a chicken around her yard in Botswana. He says more in an interview:

> That particular vision, that experience, made me think it would be good to write about a woman like her. I wondered what her story was, this woman, and I reflected upon how she probably had a very interesting past . . . I thought it would be a good idea to write about such a person, but I didn't form any particular idea or intention of doing so. The idea must have bubbled away in the subconscious . . . I don't know where the ideas come from. They're products of the subconscious. I don't actually think very much while I'm writing; I don't regard it as a very cognitive process. I sit down and it's almost as if I am in a trance. Out it comes. It's changed very little, if at all, afterwards. The subconscious is producing these ideas based on impressions and its own activity.[1]

McCall Smith's subconscious will be formed by his own experience and the culture in which he has been immersed which, to judge by the novels themselves, is a Christian one. I hope that this book will enable us to reflect theologically upon our own lives and culture.

I suggested in Chapter 1 that living the Christian life is like being involved in a drama. I drew attention to Tom Wright's analogy with performing a Shakespeare play, the last act of which has been lost, using the Scriptures and the Christian tradition (which constitute the first four acts in this analogy). Sam Wells has recently written a book on Christian ethics entitled *Improvisation* (in which Tom Wright's analogy is quoted) reflecting at some length upon the idea of seeing the Christian life as improvisation. Wells suggests that if we apply Tom Wright's analogy to the Christian story then it should be Act Four of the play in which we are involved rather than the last. This is because, as I suggested in the previous chapter, we know that God's love has triumphed in Christ and that the final outcome of the play is not in doubt: good will prevail. We are involved in the in-between time of 'already' and 'not yet', poised between the resurrection of Jesus and the final consummation of all things when he shall come again in glory. In Act One we learn that the love in the Holy Trinity overflowed in creation. God created the world and us as creatures within it for us to be in relationship with God for ever. However, God's creatures abused their freedom and chose to rebel. This is the story of the Creation and the Fall as we read it in the Bible. The second act tells of how God did not give up on the creation but chose a people with whom to be in true relationship. It is the Old Testament, a love story between God and the chosen people, the people of Israel, in which we learn of their call and the covenant God makes with them. So many relationships in our world today are characterized by contract: 'I'll do this if you do that.' A covenant is different. Someone entering into a covenant binds him or herself to do a particular thing no matter what. That is what God did to the chosen people, persevering in love for them despite the fact that they continually rebelled. However, a new act was needed in the face of this continuous rebellion, and in Act Three, the definitive act, we learn of Jesus. This is where the author enters the story. In Christ the fullness of God dwelt. Here the drama is at its most stark, where Christ is followed and then betrayed but, in his death, shows the depths of his love. That love triumphs as he rises from the dead on the third day, thereby destroying the gulf that had developed between God and the human race through sin.

Christians are in Act Four. Whereas the Jewish people thought they were in a three-act play, Creation – Israel – Messiah, this turned out not to be God's plan. Instead, through Jesus, God inaugurated Act Four in which the Church is given everything it needs to continue to be his body in the world. It was clothed with power from on high when it received the Holy Spirit. It has been given the Scriptures, made up of the apostolic witness of those who have been involved in the drama and sought to report it. It has been given baptism and the Eucharist and a host of practices to form and sustain its life. Those of us who have faith are called to use all that we have been given in the first three acts to improvise, as does Mma Ramotswe, in this fourth act. We look forward to Act Five when the triumph of God's love will be made fully manifest as all things are consummated in Christ.

As we saw in the last chapter, it is important for us to remember that we are not in the final act. The predominantly secular and 'pragmatically atheist' world in which we live in western Europe tempts us to believe that we are involved in a one-act play, that this world is all that there is. As Wells puts it: 'This life is all there is: heritage has no logical value other than in so far as it contributes to fulfilment in this life. All achievements, all results, all outcomes must be celebrated and resolved before the final whistle.'[2] This life cannot hold such a burden and nor is it meant to. The liberating thing about this is that it enables us to form a true perspective upon our lives and rejoice in the fact that this world does not have the last word. We are freed from the associated temptation of seeing this world as a one-act play and thereby exaggerating our own role in the drama, of assuming that there is no experience to learn from, no story to join, no drama to enter, a besetting sin in a society obsessed with the individual and apt to forget its collective past rather than learn from it.

The drama of the *No. 1 Ladies Detective Agency* series can be an active encouragement in reflecting upon how to lead better lives as we seek to discern our part in God's great drama in Act Four, the true context in which we are called to live out our lives. We shall not live better lives by copying Mma Ramotswe but, as I have tried to show in this book, reflecting theologically upon the series can provide us with a useful resource in attempting to dig deeper into the Christian tradition and so be enabled to make use of all the latter gives us for this life and the next.

I feel much personal empathy with McCall Smith since I, too, fell in love with southern Africa when I first went there nearly 25 years ago. I have returned as often as I can because I was hugely and positively affected by the place in general and the life of Christians within it in particular. It gave me another standard by which to look at western society, and the Church within it, and reflect theologically upon them. The books McCall Smith has written will help others to catch a glimpse of the glories of Africa. My hope is that this present volume may, through encouraging theological reflection, enable Christians to dig deep into both the novels and their faith in order to encounter Living Love and to be empowered in living love.

Afterword

ALEXANDER McCALL SMITH

It is a very strange experience for an author to read what another has written about his work. In general, I avoid this as much as possible, as I feel that it is important to write without thinking too much of what the critics say. This approach, I think, helps one to avoid self-consciousness in writing.

This wonderful book by John Inge has been an exception to my own rule. Not only have I read it, but I greatly enjoyed doing so. And this was not simply because he has been so kind to me – showing me rather more kindness than I deserve, I fear! – but because I think that he has so thoroughly understood Mma Ramotswe and the other characters in the books. He has understood, too, that which I have, perhaps subconsciously and unintentionally, been trying to say about the sort of virtue that one encounters in countries like Botswana. If the books have a message – and I do not sit down and write a message into them – then it surely must be that somebody like Mma Ramotswe has a great deal to teach us about kindness, forgiveness, and indeed about living a Christian life.

And so for me the reading of this book was a very moving experience. I have learned a great deal about how things which I simply describe as a mere chronicler relate to broader philosophical and theological issues. I shall continue for a very long time to think of what has been said in this book.

But Mma Ramotswe herself must have the last word. There she is, sipping her red bush tea in the No 1 Ladies' Detective Agency in Gaborone.

'Bishops!' she said to Mma Makutsi.

'Bishops, Mma?'

'Yes,' said Mma Ramostwe. 'I suddenly thought of bishops. But do you think that any bishops think of us?'

Mma Makutsi thought for a moment. One never knew, one simply never knew.

And so they raised their cups of bush tea in toast, and Mma Ramostwe said, 'To Bishop Trevor in Botswana, and Bishop John in England!'

And then they finished their tea and went back to work.

Notes

CHAPTER 1

1. The *Guardian*, 21 January 2003.
2. I. Murdoch, *The Sovereignty of Good*, London: Routledge and Keagan Paul, 1970, p. 101.
3. N.T. Wright 'How Can the Bible be Authoritative' in *Vox Evangelica* 21 (1991), pp. 18–19, quoted in S. Wells, *Improvisation: The Drama of Christian Ethics*, London: SPCK, 2004, p. 52.
4. Press release by the Archbishop of York, 7 December 2006.
5. Quoted by Andrew Rumsey in *Third Way*, Vol. 30, No. 1, Winter 2007, p. 29.

CHAPTER 2

1. The *Guardian*, 21 January 2003.
2. Review at www.durham21.co.uk.
3. J. Polkinghorne, *Belief in God in an Age of Science*, New Haven: Yale University Press, 1998, p. 12.
4. R. Dawkins, *River out of Eden*, London: Weidenfield and Nicholson, 1995, pp. 132–33.
5. E. Wiesel, *Night*, quoted in J. Moltmann, *The Crucified God*, London: SCM Press, 1974, p. 273.
6. J. de Gruchy, *Reconciliation: Restoring Justice*, London: SCM Press, 2002, p. 57.

CHAPTER 3

1. A. McFadyen, *Bound to Sin*, Cambridge: Cambridge University Press, 2000, p. 9.
2. McFadyen, *Bound to Sin*, p. 4.
3. T. Gorringe, *God's Just Vengeance*, Cambridge: Cambridge University Press, 1996, p. 267.
4. N. Mandela, *Long Walk to Freedom*, Little, Brown and Company, 1994, p. 559.

5. T. Merton, *The Sign of Jonas*, London: Sheldon Press, 1976, Introduction.
6. See, for example, Kestenbaum, R.; Farber, E.A.; and Sroufe, L.A. 'Individual Differences in Empathy Among Preschoolers: Relation to Attachment History' in *Empathy and Related Emotional Responses*, No. 44, San Francisco: Jossey-Bass, Inc., 1989.
7. The most well-known proponent of the view was Field Marshall Lord Slim. See. W. Slim, *Courage*, London: Cassell & Company, 1957.

CHAPTER 4

1. R. Skynner and J. Cleese, *Life and How to Survive It*, London: Methuen, 1993, p. 15.
2. Quoted in E. Carmichael, *Friendship*, London: T&T Clark, 2004, p. 138.
3. D. Bonhoeffer, *Prayers from Prison,* London: SCM Press, 1977), p. 29.
4. The No. 1 Ladies' Detective Agency Website (www. randomhouse.com/features/mccallsmith/no./.html).
5. Aelred of Rievaulx, *Spiritual Friendship*, 1.49.
6. E. Carmichael, *Friendship*, London: T&T Clark, 2004.
7. See, for example, V. Brümmer, *The Model of Love*, Cambridge, Cambridge University Press, 1993.

CHAPTER 6

1. N.T. Wright, *The Resurrection of the Son of God*, London: SPCK, 2003, p. 706.
2. J. Polkinghorne, *Quarks, Chaos and Christianity: Questions to Science and Religion*, London: SPCK, 1994, p. 92.
3. See N. Murphy, *Bodies and Souls or Animated Bodies?* Cambridge: Cambridge University Press, 2006 for a good overview of thinking in this area.
4. Polkinghorne, *Quarks, Chaos and Christianity*, p. 92.
5. T. Mwanza, *Dancing Sermons,* Edinburgh: Maclean Dubois, 2006, p. 2.

Notes

CHAPTER 7

1. Interview of McCall Smith by Dave Weich in 1998 at www. powells.com/authors/smith.html
2. Wells, *Improvisation*, p. 55.